CW00704350

·TERRA MARE·   QUE FIDE·

A VERY CANNY SCOT

A VERY CANNY SCOT

'Great' Daniel Campbell
of Shawfield & Islay 1670–1753

HIS LIFE & TIMES

Joanna Hill and Nicholas Bastin

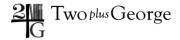 Two *plus* George

2007

Published by
Two Plus George Ltd
25 Warren Way, Barnham, West Sussex, England
twoplusgeorge.co.uk

© Joanna Hill and Nicholas Bastin, 2007

ISBN 978-0-9556228-1-6

Printed and bound in Great Britain by
The Cromwell Press, Trowbridge, Wiltshire

Endpapers:
Daniel used the crossed oars of Skipness as his seal in the early years.
In the latter part of his life Daniel used the Griffin of Islay holding the sun disc in his paws
for his seal.

Contents

Acknowledgements   vi

Introduction: A Harsh Inheritance   1
1. The Making of a Fortune   5
2. The Darien Disaster   19
3. Consolidating a Fortune; Collector of Customs   25
4. Daniel in Politics   31
5. The Equivalent and Aspects of Early Banking in Scotland   47
6. Great Daniel's Family and Properties   54
7. The Shawfield Riots   65
8. Laird of Islay   80
9. Great Daniel's Descendants   89
10. Epilogue   102

Appendices:
1. Key Members of the Campbells of Skipness, Shawfield   104
   and Islay, 1600-1900
2. Discovery of the Shawfield Manuscript   106
3. Summary of Trading Voyages from the Shawfield Manuscript   107
4. Inventory of Goods found after the Shawfield Riots   110
5. The Life and Career of Colin Campbell of   114
   Ardpatrick (1787–1858)

Bibliography   115
Index   119

Acknowledgements

We should like to thank the following for their help in researching this book: staff of the Mitchell Library, Glasgow; the National Archives, Kew; the National Archives of Scotland, Edinburgh; the British Library and the National Library of Scotland; the North Lanarkshire Museum's Archive section at Airdrie. In addition, thanks are due to Dr Henrik Klackenberg of the National Archives of Sweden; Margareta Andersson of the Stockholm City Archives; Tracey Earl, archivist, Coutts & Co.; Ruth Reed, archivist, The Royal Bank of Scotland and Mariam Yamin, archivist, Drummonds Bank together with Catriona Campbell Bourdillon, genealogist, who supplied most of the family tree and other vital information. We have also to thank Monsieur Francis Diaz, photographer, in Montsempron Libos, France for his skilful work on the old photographs which rendered them fit for publication, and to Adam Johnstone for his beautiful map and the coats of arms. Our thanks are also due to others who wish to remain anonymous; we hope they will recognise this as our expression of gratitude.

Daniel Campbell merits two pages in the *Dictionary of National Biography* due to his influence in late seventeenth- and early eighteenth-century Scottish history, but he has never previously been the subject of a biography. This may well be largely due to the fact that the family possessions became so widely dispersed following bankruptcy in the mid-nineteenth century. Despite the collection of papers in the Mitchell Archive in the Glasgow City Archives, which has preserved some fascinating details of his early trading activities, there are large parts of his life which can only be studied through other manuscripts and secondary sources. Unfortunately some gaps remain. We have, therefore, endeavoured to piece together the career of this larger-than-life figure from the numerous sources in which he is mentioned, but we do not doubt that there may be more material still hidden in dusty archives that we failed to find. We apologise in advance for any omissions deliberate or accidental.

During the course of our researches, we have found some errors in old pedigrees, which is hardly surprising given the number of Colins, Johns and Walters in every successive generation. We think we have put the record right for this small section of the vast Clan Campbell, but take full responsibility for any errors.

JOANNA HILL AND NICHOLAS BASTIN

A Harsh Inheritance

D onald Campbell was only fifteen years old when he heard the news of his uncle Colin's violent death in 1685. Despite a successful plea for clemency, the messenger had returned too late and Colin's body swung from the gallows tree in front of Inveraray Castle together with those of 16 fellow Campbell clansmen. Colin was at least spared the barbarity inflicted on Major John Campbell, who had his arms hacked off before he was strung up. Their crime was to support their Clan Chief, Archibald 9th Earl of Argyll, in his flawed and hopeless rebellion against King James VII (II). This summary justice was not unusual in the Highlands of Scotland in the seventeenth century, a time when right had to be matched with might and the weak often did not survive. To subdue the Campbells and punish them for their rebellion, the King sent the Marquess of Atholl to ravage Argyll, a commission which he executed with vigour and brutality.

Donald's grief would have been exacerbated by the continuing threat to his father's life. Walter Campbell, Captain of Skipness, was held under suspicion of involvement in the same rebellion. He was imprisoned with other senior members of the clan in the fastness of Edinburgh Castle—a world away from Donald's Argyll home: Skipness Castle on the north eastern tip of Kintyre. Skipness was one of the most strategic castles of the west coast of Scotland, its position giving it command of the sea routes to Arran, Bute and the entrance to Loch Fyne, as well as guarding the gateway from the highlands to Glasgow and the lowlands. Large and historic, the thirteenth-century castle was also rough and rudimentary when compared with contemporary houses of Lowland, or English, gentry; but it was Donald's home. Any semblance of domesticity would have vanished when it was attacked and captured by the Marquess of Atholl's troops and, although Donald would doubtless have been cheered by the subsequent news of its recapture by the Campbell militia, it was clear that further retribution was unavoidable. When Atholl had finally reduced Argyll to a smoking ruin, with the Earl of Argyll captured and beheaded, it was ordered that the castle be razed to the ground. Fortunately, with relative calm restored, the Government felt secure enough to release prisoners, such as Donald's father, who must have returned to find their families living in very straitened circumstances. Walter subsequently successfully overturned the Government's order to destroy the castle, but, in return, he committed to leave Skipness and went to live with his third wife's family in Bute. After 180 years of occupation, the family would never inhabit the castle itself again.

The third* of five brothers—Angus, John, Donald, Matthew and Robert— Donald had grown up in the harsh reality of life in the highlands of Scotland in the seventeenth century with its violence and insecurity. He also knew that, thanks to the laws of primogeniture, he could not expect an inheritance from his family; he had to make his own way in the world. The bond with his brothers was strong and they formed successful partnerships in their dealings across the globe, but Donald became the leader, by far the toughest and certainly the most successful. With the rugged spine of Kintyre rising behind Skipness, the natural prospect lies across the sea to the south east and it is easy to understand why these young Campbells had such a natural affinity with the sea, which would later be the foundation of Daniel's fortune.

This turbulent childhood motivated Donald and his brothers to take great risks, both personal and financial, to break the law when it seemed expedient, and to stand up for themselves. That Donald was pragmatic and ambitious can be seen in his adoption at an early age, of the anglicised name of Daniel, which he used ever after. The changes that he witnessed throughout his long life were profound and he was to play a key role in many of the most important Scottish affairs of his day. He harnessed his prodigious energies to become one of Scotland's richest men, laying the foundation of Glasgow's trading empire. He was also a Commissioner for the Treaty of Union and one of the few Scottish commoners to sign the Act of Union of Scotland and England in 1707. He subsequently become a pillar of the Hanoverian regime and such a close friend to Sir Robert Walpole, that when his grand new house in Glasgow was destroyed in one of the most serious civil riots of the eighteenth century, it rocked the establishment and prompted the direct intervention of both the Prime Minister and the King.

Known as 'Great' Daniel, he lived up to this epithet in every way: both in physical size—he was six-and-a-half feet tall—and in his wealth and influence. Nevertheless, it has proved hard to find images of him. One painting suggests a proud man exuding authority, the typical Whig of his era (see page 18).† A second portrait, in a private collection, is somewhat softer but still shows a man of charisma and influence (see colour plate facing page 58). Dressed in an expensive blue velvet coat and fashionable high wig, he is not in the flush of youth. His face shows strength and self-confidence; his eyes stare out of the picture and hold your gaze. Despite the fine clothes and fleshy face, there is a palpable core of steel to this middle-aged man, who was energetic, canny and certainly unscrupulous when occasion arose.

---

* His date of birth is uncertain and it is possible that brother Matthew could have been the third brother and Daniel the fourth.

† It was the property of Captain Walter Campbell in the late nineteenth century, but has now vanished and there is only an illustration of it from Constance, Lady Russell's book, *Three Generations of Fascinating Women*.

While ambitious and undoubtedly a pillar of the establishment, Daniel never forsook his roots; he not only remained committed to Scotland but also to the Highlands, despite their dangerous and violent character. This was in sharp contrast to many members of the Scottish aristocracy who had effectively emigrated to Court in London and never visited their Scottish estates, merely milking them for as much as their factor could squeeze from the tenants. Throughout his career Daniel had close dealings with his fellow clansmen and unashamedly used them as partners in his trading ventures, generally to their mutual advantage. Clan ties were strong and enduring and carried a weight which now, with the passage of time, can be hard to entirely fathom.

Daniel's upbringing would have been unimaginable to his English contemporaries at the London court, and yet in due course, he managed to straddle both worlds with great success. A firm friend and an inveterate enemy, he unquestionably always had an eye for the main chance and chose to disregard conventions or laws where he found them an impediment to his plans. This self-reliance bred many enemies, particularly among the Jacobites or the lowland gentry, such as the families of Hamilton and Montrose, who resented his success, particularly when he encroached on what they considered their territory. That he disregarded this pressure, sometimes from among the most powerful men and women of the day, reflects the fortitude and strength that must have lain at his core. His resolute support for the Hanoverians was surely born out of hatred for the Stewarts and what they had done to his immediate family. Indeed, this antipathy and the memory of the destruction they had suffered must have lain behind his decision to erect a monument to his uncle, Colin, nearly seventy years

Monument to Colin Campbell by Frews Bridge, Inveraray Castle. (Photograph: Nicholas Bastin)

after the event. This monument which now stands just a few yards from the main entrance to Inveraray Castle,* commemorates the sacrifice of Colin and his fellow clansmen. The inscription reads:

> Sacred to the memory of Colin, brother German to Walter Campbell of Skipness, who among others tenacious of Evangelical religion and the liberty of the people, yielded to an unjust death in the year of our Lord 1685. His uprightness, though tried by adverse circumstances, in a sad time, has grounds for praise. Prospera luxoritur linguis animisque favete— Propitious dawn is breaking give support with word and thought.†

Great Daniel's unwavering opposition to the Jacobites was a constant theme throughout his life, and can be contrasted with the vacillation of many others in a society in which many members always waited to see which way the wind was blowing before committing or hedged their bets by backing both sides. Even during the darkest moments of the '45 rebellion, when it must have seemed that Bonnie Prince Charlie had Scotland in his grip, Daniel never considered switching sides.

While a shrewd merchant with an eye for money-making schemes and certainly one who understood the value of money, Daniel enjoyed his wealth and position. On occasion, he spent freely: building one of Scotland's earliest and grandest Palladian mansions in Glasgow and creating some of its finest gardens at his Woodhall estate. The money he spent on Islay was to show the least financial return but it portrays him as a perhaps unexpectedly enlightened landlord.

Despite his high profile and undoubted success, Daniel remains something of an enigma; most of his personal papers have disappeared over the intervening centuries. However, enough material remains in scattered archives to paint a colourful picture of one of eighteenth-century Scotland's great survivors, who triumphed over many adversities and who took tremendous personal risks to advance himself, his family and his beliefs in the face of ever present physical and political dangers.

---

* The original castle lay a few yards from the present building.
† Although a Duncan Campbell of Skipness is credited with erecting this monument it was, in fact, Daniel who commissioned and paid for it although it was not erected until just after his death in 1753.

1

The Making of a Fortune

The destruction in Argyll wrought by the Atholl raid in 1685 may have been a blessing in disguise for Daniel, as it undoubtedly forced him and his brothers (with the exception of Angus, who inherited the family estate of Skipness) to seek opportunity elsewhere. Daniel was apprenticed to Robert Campbell in Glasgow, a merchant and Dean of Guild, in the middle 1680s. The role of Dean of Guild had been established in 1605 when the people of Glasgow were suffering losses owing to 'strangers usurping their commercial privileges'.[*] They consequently nominated a body of merchants and craftsmen under a Dean of Guild to protect their interests. This apprenticeship was a stroke of genius, forging Daniel in the career which would be the foundation of his success. He rapidly learned the ropes of trade from his master, with whom he was already trading to the Baltic ports in the late 1680s.

Whether is was intention or serendipity that led Walter to apprentice Daniel in Glasgow, he could not have chosen a better location or time to do so. The river Clyde forms a natural, virtually horizontal entry way into the heart of Scotland. Historically, it led the country's people to look west to the Atlantic and America for their foreign trade in the late seventeenth and eighteenth century, whereas the east coast looked more naturally towards Holland and the Baltic. The city of Glasgow had risen rapidly from being only the fourth or fifth burgh in Scotland to its place as the undisputed number two. One estimate says that the city doubled in size during the seventeenth century and certainly by around 1700, it had a population of approximately 12,000. Glasgow was a pioneer in the first Scottish trade across the Atlantic, largely thanks to a small number of merchants who were prepared to 'stand the risks of new ventures to unknown markets'.[†] Between them, Edinburgh and Glasgow contributed around 45 per cent of the taxes levied on all royal Burghs, so far 'from being the stagnant little market town' imagined by Smout and many others, Glasgow was already a successful burgh with 'wealth and confidence'.[‡]

At the end of the seventeenth century, more than half of Scotland's trade was with non-English markets. Despite the fact that Scotland shared a king

---

[*]   *Three Generations of Fascinating Women*, p. 158.
[†]   Smout, *Scottish Trade on the Eve of Union*.
[‡]   Smout, Scottish Historical Society, No. 143, vol. XLV11, April 1968.

Skipness Castle (Photograph: Nicholas Bastin)

with England, however, it was precluded by the English Navigation Acts from trading with the English colonies. The embargoes against Scottish trading naturally resulted in a highly successful and widespread smuggling trade, ensuring that prices for items such as tobacco undercut their English rivals. It is possible that as much as half of all imports in Glasgow from the colonies of Virginia and Maryland managed to evade the payment of duty. Merchants connived with Customs and Excise officers—sometimes, as was the case with Daniel later in his career, these could be one and the same person.

Prior to the Glorious Revolution of 1689, Scottish trade to North America had been so tiny in quantity that it is surprising that England evinced such antagonism and took such heavy-handed measures to protect its own trade. The English went to extraordinary lengths to ensure that the Scots could not become serious competition where trans-Atlantic trade was concerned, and the Scottish merchants had to devise crafty methods in order to succeed and profit from the lucrative trade that was opening up across the ocean. Unfortunately, the often quoted Register of 1692 cannot be considered reliable since too many of those involved in compiling it had a vested interest in demonstrating the poverty of Scottish shipping. There are extant records of Glasgow ships trading directly with the American colonies and, prior to Union, Daniel certainly did so, but before 1707 they often chartered English ships to mask Scottish ownership of cargo. Scottish merchants also frequently used Whitehaven in Cumbria as their port of entry and/or exit in a ruse designed to conceal true cargo ownership. This led to Whitehaven thriving as a port at the end of the seventeenth century and during the first half of the eighteenth before sliding back into a quieter, less prosperous way of life once Scotland was at liberty to trade legally.

As very few ships were armed, they frequently sailed in convoy for security against privateers, the English Navy and at the frequent times of war, the French Navy. One convoy of ships, all Scottish, which sailed from Whitehaven for Virginia on 9 June 1700, lists the size of ships and the number of men on board; the crews ranged from the largest which carried 28 sailors to the smallest with only two.

Such measures were not foolproof. In 1689 at the age of about nineteen, Daniel petitioned the Earl of Nottingham, the English Secretary of State, for recompense following the seizure of a cargo from the ship *St Andrew*.[*] There is also a memorial to Lord Melville, another English Secretary of State, concerning two guard ships: the 18-gun *Pelican* and the 12-gun *Jannet*. These two frigates had been leased by the Navy to act as protection against French privateers and which were owned by the Provost of Glasgow and Robert Campbell, Dean of Guild. (In fact, Daniel owned a share of the *Jannet*, the major portion belonging to his old apprentice master.) Unfortunately, the two captains mistook a distant flotilla for that of Commander Rooke[†] of the English Navy and approached to make contact. Too late, they realised their error, and the French privateers sank the *Jannet* and took the *Pelican* as their prize. The battle between the French and the two frigates was so fierce that it lasted for seven hours and it is on record that only 30 sailors survived from the Scottish ships.

Such obstacles to Scottish trade certainly contributed to Daniel's resolve to try and make his fortune on the other side of the Atlantic. His decision may have been influenced by the embargo created at a Meeting of the Estates in 1689[‡] which prevented all vessels at Western Scottish ports from sailing for Ireland in order to bring Jacobites to Scotland. Daniel sailed to Boston in 1689 or 1690 as part owner of a cargo. His brother, John, and a cousin, Duncan, were already established in New England when Daniel joined them. Although he had already been exporting linen (at that time Scotland's biggest export to the Colonies[§]) to the Americas, it was no easy matter for Scottish merchants, with their ships running the gauntlet of both the English Navy and greedy French privateers. According to Admiral Sir George Rooke, these tiny vessels were also vulnerable to the weather and many were lost due 'to going out too late in the year'.

Daniel was one of the Glasgow merchants who chose to defy the Navigation Acts and, from around 1690, was involved in a highly dangerous but, overall,

---

[*] NAS, GD26/7/276 and GD26/7/260.
[†] Later to become Admiral Sir George Rooke.
[‡] The Convention of Estates was a body that sat when Parliament was not in session. It had the power to pass temporary legislation that would have to be ratified by Parliament at a later date.
[§] Shawfield MS, No. 38.

very lucrative trade with North America and the West Indies. The west coast of Scotland was ideally placed for voyages to north America. There was much less risk that ships would be taken by privateers or the English navy as they left the Clyde and headed out across the Atlantic; their English competitors had to brave the dangers of the English Channel and then the seas around Ireland, all of which offered excellent opportunities for their enemies, principally French privateers. This route also added approximately two week to each voyage. There were already many Scottish immigrants in the English colonies in North America and Daniel found people in the settlements very happy to deal with him and his ships. Scotsmen liked to deal with fellow Scots and the factors in many colonies were either family or at least fellow clansmen. Some of these were salaried, but most worked on a percentage of the cargoes they arranged. Daniel had a natural and enduring partnership with his brothers, John, Matthew and Robert, on whom he could rely completely. They extended their network in partnerships with their cousin Dugald Campbell of Kilberrie, other cousins such as Archibald and Alexander Campbell and Clan Campbell contacts in the New World and beyond. Clan ties were strong and family ties even stronger, this helped to create a network of shrewd operators that were happy to sail close to the wind and take great risks for their mutual benefit.

The brothers bought small ships in New England and traded goods along the eastern seaboard to the settlements of Maryland, Virginia, North Carolina and eventually the Caribbean. These ships carried linen and herring from Scotland and returned laden with sugar and tobacco. Daniel's letters demonstrate that Glasgow merchants were trading in these commodities much earlier and on a somewhat larger scale than had previously been thought. Much of the tobacco was re-exported to Germany, the Netherlands and the Baltic. Daniel can legitimately be considered as one of the original tobacco lords; previous histories have often implied that the import of tobacco did not start until later in the eighteenth century. It is, of course, perfectly true that these early years saw only relatively small amounts being brought into Scotland but records of the Chesapeake colony demonstrate that the trade was generally thriving, although always subject to fluctuation according to poor harvests and bad weather.[*] Governor Nicholson of Maryland sent lists to the Government in London of Scotsmen trading 'illegally'.[†] Amongst the names is an Alexander 'Camboll'[‡] and a Matthew 'Cammell'[§] together with other names that appear in Daniel's papers. The Governor asked King William to provide the Colony with two or three small armed ships to patrol along the coast and river mouths checking on all ships passing out or into the bay within the Cape of Virginia and to inspect the Collector's books to discover forged dockets or

[*] NA TI/326/21, TI/276B/372.
[†] NA, Colonial Series CO5/714, CO 5/1 308; 'Scottish Trade with the Plantations', *William and Mary Quarterly*, series 3, vol. ii, 1957, p. 183.
[‡] Alexander Campbell was a fellow clansman who skippered Daniel's ships.
[§] Almost certainly Daniel's brother, Matthew.

certificates. The ships frequently carried at least two different sets of papers to cover such contingencies. The Scots certainly had a lot to contend with, but they managed rather well considering all these impediments!

The Campbells also had ships built in New England, and the specifications survive of one that was commissioned by Daniel from a shipwright called Rowland Storey in Boston.* The ship was 51 feet long with a 12-foot rake at the stern; she was nine feet deep in the hold and displaced 100 tonnes. The cost was £406 10s in New England money. This was costed on the basis of £3-5 a 'tunn'. Although this was not a very sizeable ship in modern terms, many of those used by the brothers were even smaller. This enabled them to enter those harbours and river mouths where larger vessels could not go and, as a result, they could avoid having to pay Customs dues. Of course, it carried risks too: for example, the ketch *Prosperous*, captained by Ebenezer Chapin and carrying a cargo of tobacco, which she had just taken on board in the 'Pocomok' river, was taken and ransomed.† The cost of release was high—but this was all part of the game.

Detailed planning was essential for Scottish-owned vessels to avoid both the English fleet and, most importantly, English customs duty. Included among Daniel's papers is a long and most precise set of instructions, given in October 1696 to James Robison, Supercargo,‡ on how to avoid customs.§ These instructions were designed to ensure that he evaded both privateers and English naval vessels, and managed to bring back a profitable cargo that had not paid English duty. Six Glasgow merchants, including Daniel, each put up £100 to finance this particular voyage and the instructions cover several pages.

Firstly Robison was to ship a cargo of linen to England, on which he would pay duty at the port of Carlisle. He was then to proceed to London, where he was to find a ship sailing for either New York or Boston, preferably the latter. He would also purchase more goods in London. On arrival in New England, he was to sell the goods and buy a 'half worn ship'. He was also to seek out Captain Matthew Campbell, Daniel's brother, and ask him to subscribe a further £100, giving him a one-seventh share.

Once Robison had purchased the ship, he was to buy a load of goods suitable for trade with Maryland—probably sugar, salt and molasses—after which he would sail south. On arrival in Maryland, he was to dispatch the Captain to 'the Collector' (of Excise) who was to be invited on board and treated lavishly. The Collector would demand that they had a bondsman and Robison was to say that he would find one but that being a stranger it might take a little time. The ship was then to be loaded with the return

---

*   Shawfield MS, No. 38.
†   *Prosperous* appears in Shawfield MS, Nos 41, 44, 45, 66, 67.
‡   Supercargos were responsible for managing the buying and selling of goods carried. Sometimes transactions were effected by barter. Subsequently, Captains took over this role.
§   Shawfield MS, No. 101.

cargo—tobacco—and the Captain was to 'persuade'* an English agent to put his company's name on the papers confirming that the shipment was heading for Bideford in Devon. Robison was explicitly told to sign nothing himself— 'give nothing under your hand'.

Once these formalities had been completed, Robison was to find a convoy sailing north. He was by no means to sail off by himself, since, as the war was still continuing, the English fleet of King William and the French fleet of Louis XIV would be on the prowl. When the convoy was sufficiently far to the north, Robison was to tell the Master of the convoy that he must leave his protection since he needed to obtain his orders at 'Kellburn Road', which is another name for the Port of Glasgow. Robison was then to sail to the West Coast of Scotland and proceed through the sounds of Mull and Islay and on round Kintyre to the Clyde. We must assume that the voyage was a success and that this careful strategy had been employed and refined during previous crossings of the Atlantic.

Daniel and his ships had many an adventure and he did, indeed, lose several to the French. In 1696, he applied to the Admiralty for compensation for some of his losses. His petition covered the loss of three ships, the *Recovery*, the *Prosperous* and the *James*. Cargoes on board all three had been lost but the 'bottoms' of two of the ships had evidently been ransomed. The loss was estimated at £2,000. According to correspondence from Argyll and the Duke of Queensberrie [sic] 'favour to be shown to merchants thereby ... doe therefore approve the Tacksmen of HM Revenue to allow the sum of £700.00'. While this petition was dated 1696, it was not until 11 years later, on the eve of the signing of the Act of Union in 1707, that Daniel finally received payment of this £700; no doubt a sweetener to a Scottish Commissioner for the Union.

In 1694, Daniel sailed back home to Scotland from America in one of his most frequently mentioned ships, the aptly named *Adventure*. The same year, his brother Matthew, known as 'of Orgaig'—one of the Skipness home farms—is recorded as being the Captain of a 22-gun ship sailing to Cádiz and this voyage appears to have been undertaken as a quasi-Naval operation. Matthew was a successful and apparently fearless skipper, sailing ships both for the family and for the Scottish Navy and joining Daniel in many trading enterprises.

On returning home, Daniel was made a burgess of Glasgow. This acknowledged the fact that he had already achieved a certain success and could demonstrate that he had made money. From this date on there is no further mention of Daniel crossing the Atlantic; he appears to have stayed at home directing operations. His marriage in 1695 to Margaret Leckie, the daughter of another Glasgow merchant, John Leckie of Newlands, Renfrew and Glasgow, may have also been a reason for ending his travels. She brought him a dowry of *c.*£10,000 Scots (approximately £850 sterling). We know little of this lady

---

* By dint of bribery.

except that she bore him six children. Some of her household bills are included in the Shawfield Manuscript; they include orders for simple requirements such as children's clothes and shoes, groceries, etc. She died in 1711.

Trading life continued to be full of drama and risk since Scottish ships did not suffer only at the hands of the French. In 1695, one of Daniel's ships,[*] the *James*, was on a winter voyage from the Canaries laden with the local wine, when she was attacked by St Malo privateers. She took shelter in Port Leaven, Cornwall, where the inhabitants 'looted her cargo and rig, stripped her crew naked'[†] and destroyed the ship. It is a classic story of old Cornish wreckers. Between 1688 and 1697, the St Malo privateers were responsible for taking 3,384 merchantmen and 162 escorting men-o'-war; a truly amazing statistic which demonstrates the real threat they posed to trade.[‡]

In 1696, the *Adventure* is recorded as sailing for the Caribbean under the command of fellow clansman, Archibald Campbell.[§] Archibald's accounts include the mention of the sale of 12 servants; they fetched £12 Scots each. However, it is not clear as to whether these were true slaves or indentured servants who had agreed to work for a fixed period to fund their escape from the appalling poverty in Scotland.

In the same year, we read of the *Lillie* loading at Montrose. She took on board 112 'servants' and hoped to pick up some more 'boys' in Orkney. It seems that people were prepared to work as indentured servants for a few years to pay for their passage in the hope of a better life in the long term. Some ship owners contracted with both the English and Scottish governments to transport consignments of prisoners and undesirable elements; these were carried in shackles from Greenock and Port Glasgow to Virginia and the Carolinas.[¶]

There exist several letters sent in 1699 from the Caribbean islands of 'St Ustatia' (better known as St Eustatia) and from St Christopher (known today as St Kitts). St Eustatia, or the Golden Rock, is a small island and a Dutch Crown colony. Discovered by Columbus in 1493, in Daniel's day St Eustatia was a free port and thus a very busy trading centre where up to 100 ships at a time could be found in the anchorage. Merchant ships plying to and fro needed to be very vigilant since, although the island was a duty free port, the English Navy treated harshly any ships carrying goods on which duty had not been paid.

Europeans in the Caribbean suffered from many tropical sicknesses and Daniel's agent wrote in August 1699 of the death of many of the inhabitants, including John Kerr, Captain of the *Adventure*. He added that he had found a replacement, Captain John Howell: 'he is in part a stranger to us but do hope he will acquit himself like an honest man'.[**] The *Adventure*'s cargo

---

[*]   He had a half share, the rest being owned by James Taillyour.

[†]   Shawfield MS; Eric J..Graham, *A Maritime History of Scotland*.

[‡]   MacIntyre, *The Privateers*, London 1975.

[§]   Shawfield MS, No. 120.

[¶]   Graham, *A Maritime History of Scotland*, p. 49.

[**]   Shawfield MS, No. 122.

contained interesting items such as beeswax and elephant teeth (probably tusks—indicating that the ship had come to the Caribbean via Guinea). It is the only time such items are mentioned in Daniel's papers. However, the very next letter dated that year, announced that Captain Howell had proved an expensive disaster. The *Adventure* had arrived safely in New York, but Captain Howell had 'disposed and converted to his own use the elephants' teeth ... and was daily entering into extravagant charges which would tend to the ruine of the shipp'. The agent said that he had sent a Power of Attorney to friends in New York instructing them to call the Captain to account and to secure the vessel until further orders were received.

A further important factor when trading with the Caribbean was that, since the Scottish-owned ships were built of wood that was not as tough as teak or ironwood, they were prone to attack by a voracious type of snail which thrived in the warm Caribbean waters. It was therefore always important to turn the ships around as fast as possible when offloading and taking on a cargo.

The final letter of this period is interesting: the agent received word from New York that the whole crew of the *Adventure*, save for four or five men, had gone home with the 'Caledonians by whom you will have a more perfect account that we can at present give you'.[*] This refers to the ship the *Caledonia* which had sailed from Caledonia (as the settlement on Darien had been named) on the isthmus of Panama with some of the unfortunate settlers. She had reached New York in a very battered condition and had subsequently sailed from New York on 9 November. Fewer than 300 souls arrived back in Scotland out of the several thousand who had set sail with such optimism. (The Darien Disaster is covered in the next chapter.)

Did Daniel Campbell deal in slaves? Since there are at least three mentions of slaves in the Shawfield Manuscript, we must assume that he did, at least on occasion. In January 1701 he wrote to James Crosse, Supercargo of the *Hopewell*, referring to the sale of the 'few slaves for ready money'.[†] This letter also refers to the death of Alexander Woodrop, a fellow Scot, who had succumbed to the deadly fever sweeping through the Caribbean islands and Daniel added that he hoped 'you will find some of our friends still alive in Nevis'. A second letter to Crosse in 1702 refers to the 'effects of the sale of the negresses in St Kitts'.[‡] This period marked the beginning of the sugar industry in the Caribbean and there was a huge demand for labour. The summary of Daniel's trading activities, mentions slaves at three different times: in 1696, 1700 and 1702.

A major export from the West Indian islands was, of course, sugar and as owner of a 'sugar house' in Glasgow, Daniel was well positioned to make spirits which were also highly marketable. There were four sugar houses in

---

[*]   Shawfield MS, No. 129.
[†]   *Ibid.*, No. 241.
[‡]   *Ibid.*, No. 224.

Glasgow including Daniel's—the South Sugar House—which was established around 1700.* The pre-existing sugar houses had already been operating for some years and the arrival of Daniel's seems to have affected their trade; Daniel would not undertake such an enterprise if he did not consider it likely to be a profitable one! He had applied for a licence to set up a distillery in Glasgow and in March 1701 John Metcalfe, one of his agents, wrote from London† informing him that he had found a well qualified distiller, William Walker, who was prepared to work for him, subject to adequate payment. Some of the spirits distilled in Glasgow were shipped to Guinea, from where slaves may have been collected in what was known as the 'triangular trade' and transported on to the Caribbean. However, there is little else in the Shawfield Manuscript to support this.‡ The sugar houses were initially only permitted to process 28 tuns free of duty but subsequently were granted the status of a 'manufactory' and as such were free of tax and duty. They processed the raw sugar known as 'muscado' which arrived in Glasgow as sticky brown or grey crystals. It was claimed during the wars with France that between 1707 and 1715 the Glasgow houses distilled half a million gallons! Their success in this trade also served to cut out the purchase of sugar from the Dutch and drastically reduced the quantity of good French brandy that was imported.

From trading solely with the English colonies in America and the West Indies, Daniel's voyages began to find new markets. He shipped salt herring to Poland and was asked for more; he shipped wool and dark tobacco to Hamburg, but was told that his wool was too dirty and he was not to send any more unless it was clean, 'the wool I cannot sell being so full of filth'. Wool was sold by weight and clearly if it was 'full of filth' it would weigh—and cost—considerably more.

During this period, Daniel's fearless brother and business partner Matthew Campbell of Orgaig embarked on a career in the Scottish Navy, in which he had many adventures as Captain of the *Dumbarton Castle*,§ commissioned in June 1703 to protect the Scottish coastline from 'the sound of Mulle [*sic*] in the Highlands to the Mulle of Galloway and from thence the length of Lambie Island near Dubline'¶ at the renewal of the war with France 'to secure the trade of Scotland from the insults of French privateers'.

In May 1705, Matthew wrote to the Earl of Seafield, Lord High Chancellor of Scotland, describing his capture of a French privateer: 'after some small

---

* Smout, *Economic History Review*, series 2, vol. 14, 1961.

† Shawfield MS, No. 204.

‡ Calendar of Treasury Papers (1714-19), vol. CCVIII, includes a petition from Daniel Campbell and John Graham dated September 1715 asking for an exemption from Customs Duty for the three sugar houses. A further entry in 1717 says that the Barons of the Exchequer have not yet reached a decision.

§ This consisted of three ships.

¶ Register of the Privy Council of Scotland, Seafield Correspondence.

conflict she surrendered having killed his Lieutenant and wounded severalls of his men'. The ship was almost certainly the *Aime Marie* which carried eight guns and 62 men—a useful prize. Matthew brought the ship into Greenock on 28 May and was anxious to know what was to be done with her and with the prisoners, whose maintenance was proving a great expense. He also needed to take the *Dumbarton Castle* out of the water to have her hull scraped. The prisoners were eventually to be exchanged but arrangements for these exchanges frequently took months.

Matthew was clearly not a man to be messed with and he had another considerable success in 1706,* when he captured a St Malo privateer, the *St Peter and St Paul*, together with that ship's own prize, the *Happy Entrance of Dublin*. It is unclear as to whether or not he was acting as an individual on this occasion, since the State Papers of Scotland Warrant Books lists the *Royal Mary* and the *Royal William* as the two men-o'-war protecting the coast of Scotland and makes no mention of Matthew Campbell. We do know from Daniel's correspondence with John Campbell of the Bank (see Chapter 5) in 1708 that Matthew had been taken prisoner by the French at that time.[†]

In 1710, Daniel sent his youngest half-brother, Robert, to New England to supervise the construction of a new ship. Robert's mother was Anne Stewart of Ardmaleish, his father's third wife and the sister of the Earl of Bute, reflecting the family's growing social status. Robert was to be the skipper and the ship was probably the *Expedition* galley which was owned in partnership with a Matthew Crawford. The ship was commissioned from Messrs Andrew and Jonathan Belchar and was to be 'a good handsome merchantman'.[‡] Robert does not seem to have been a success at sea and was dispatched to Stockholm by 1711, where he became a prominent member of the merchant community and a partner in the trading firm Campbell, Jarratt[§] and Dobson. Daniel shipped 'bright' tobacco to Sweden with the principal return cargo from the Baltic being bar iron and, sometimes, timber. Robert was also apparently 'the Stockholm correspondent of Henry Norris, one of London's premier Baltic merchants'.[¶] Norris was evidently also agent for Abraham Spooner, the largest ironmonger in the West Midlands in the 1720s and '30s, and this gave Robert Campbell entry into a very lucrative business. Since Norris and Daniel were also frequently in partnership, there is not much doubt that Daniel also profited from this trade.

---

* NAS HCAS AC/8/61 and AC9/210.

† Matthew's first wife was Magdalene Kinloch, daughter of Sir Francis Kinloch, and his second was Agnes Campbell. He had two daughters by his first wife and a son, John, described as a 'natural born fool', by his second. Matthew Campbell died in 1721.

‡ Shawfield MS, 464r.

§ John Jarratt had come from Hull. He was to be a partner of the British Factory in Stockholm some years later.

¶ A paper given by Goran Ryden of the University of Uppsala, at the annual conference of the Economic History Society at Reading University 31 March-2 April 2006 entitled 'Swedish Economic History and the New Atlantic Economy'.

Correspondence also refers to shipments of wine and brandy to Stockholm, with a letter from Robert Campbell's company clerk asking for 10-20 tons of good 'Boardeaux claret, brandy and the rest of the strongest white wine'. A large number of Scots had settled in Sweden at the beginning of the eighteenth century, and Robert appears to have been one of the successes.[*]

There are records of a large quantity of wine being shipped from Bordeaux, including some wine from the Lot valley known as Cahors. The bill of lading describes one shipment as consisting of two tons of claret, a quantity of white wine, brandy and vinegar. The wine shippers also sent some of the famous 'prunes d'Agen' which are still to be found all over the world. He apologised that the prunes were smaller than the previous year due to the lack of rain. Madeira was well situated for taking on water as well as cargoes of Madeira wine en route to and from the Caribbean. Salt beef was a popular outward bound cargo. Today, one would consider barrels of salted herrings a poor type of fare in the West Indies but evidently in the early eighteenth century it was highly popular, being Scotland's second-largest export. It was a cargo that kept well, although it was not unknown for the herrings to go off in extreme tropical heat!

Disaster was never far away; for example, a letter records a load of sugar being brought into St Christopher that was completely ruined by sea water washing over the boat and through an open hatch, so that the ship almost foundered and the whole cargo was lost. Severe winter weather frequently caused delays and often forced ships to return to port. In all, it was a very tough business which resulted in charges for insurance of which Daniel was frequently complaining.

Further evidence that the long Campbell arm was reaching new and far off places is provided in an account of trading with Archangel.[†] At the time there appears to have been a Russian embargo on foreign ships using the port of St Petersburg.

Italy may seem close to hand today, but it was a long voyage in the early years of the eighteenth century. In 1708, Daniel's cousin Dugald Campbell of Kilberrie,[‡] skipper and joint owner of the *Neptune*, sends details of a shipment from 'Port Po'.[§] This was the port at the mouth of the river Po that served as the gateway to Tuscany and Florence in particular. Dugald made several successful voyages there. Items varied; amongst them were large quantities of both red and white 'Florence' wine provided by Ottavio Landi of Florence, white chianti (muscadello), coffee, almonds, jars of virgin oil from Lucca and milled rice. There is also mention of four barrels of wine that had been

---

[*] By 1750, the Swedes had become jealous of their success and started to squeeze them out of trade by taxing cargoes carried in foreign ships very highly.

[†] The ship *Esler* sailed there in 1706/7, MS 300.

[‡] Dugald Campbell of Kilberrie. He also served in the Navy following Union.

[§] Shawfield MS, No. 345.

Grave stone of Dugald Campbell of Kilberry, Kilberry Castle (Photograph: Nicholas Bastin)

consumed by the sailors who were engaged in rinsing out the barrels! In all, it appears that they were shipping much the same goods three hundred years ago as one might expect today.

A later letter written by Dugald and sent from Livorno (Leghorn), informs Daniel that he has encountered 'misfortunes on my last voyage'.[*] It appears that he was sailing from Egypt on the *Concord* when she was attacked by a 54-gun ship, forcing her on to 'the coast of Barbary'. Despite six feet of water in the hold, Dugald held the attacker off for four days 'resolving not to strike nor surrender to his boats at last he [the attacker] got a small privateer to his assistance which had water to alongest our side'. Poor Dugald still hoped to get his ship back but asks Daniel how much it was insured for. He ends his letter saying 'I trouble you too much at present with an history of my misfortunes'. We do not hear if he ever recovered the *Concord* but it seems unlikely. An anecdote relates that Dugald was captured by the Turks, spent some time in a Turkish prison and was rescued by a beautiful Turkish lady![†] If this is true, it may have happened following the loss of his ship on 'the barbary coast'.

Following the Act of Union in 1707, it became much easier for Scottish merchants to trade with other parts of the world, since they no longer had to prevent their cargoes being taken by the English. There was, however, still plenty to contend with and insurance costs were a constant subject of correspondence between Daniel and Henry Norris in London, his partner in many ventures. One reference to the high cost of insurance negotiated by Norris, gives an account of goods to be carried on the *Houston* galley bound for Cork, Madeira and Antigua. Insured for a 'capital of £600 at 3% plus policy plus commission' the premium amounted to £21. Norris added, 'they do not care to insure on the Guinea adventure under 10%'. This letter was one of the very last to be found in the collection of papers that make up the

---

* Letter from Dugald Campbell to Daniel, in Shawfield MS, No. 374. See also following references.

† A tale related by the late historian Marion Campbell of Kilberrie.

Shawfield manuscript and was dated 5 December 1719. The manuscript as it is today, is plainly only a very small part of Daniel's business papers and the assertion by John Francis Campbell in the 1860s that someone had taken the most interesting items at some time, is probably true.

Sir William Seton wrote in 1700:

> So soon as a merchant hath scraped together a piece of money, perhaps to the value of 4000 or 5000lb sterl. instead of employing it for promoting trade or by projecting any new thing, that may be serviceable to his country, and to the augmenting of his stock nothing will satisfy him but the laying out of it upon a land estate, for having the honour to make his son a laird, that is an idle person, who can find as many methods in spending his father's money, as he had of gaining it.[*]

While few Scottish merchants had sufficient funds to buy a really sizeable property at the time, Daniel Campbell was an exception. He doubtless regarded land ownership as both a sound investment and as a step up on the social ladder and consequently decided to invest his early success in his first lairdship, that of Clochfin just outside the town of Lochend (now Campbeltown) in Kintyre. There is a record of a payment of his feus to John Campbell, Chamberlain to the Duke of Argyll in 1702.[†] It was probably a small property and was held from the Duke of Argyll. By the time that he was elected to the Scottish Parliament the following year, he styled himself as 'of Ardentinnie' and there are no further mentions of Clochfin. He had acquired Ardentinnie from his first cousin and it had additional significance for Daniel. As the ancestral seat of the senior branch of the Campbells of Skipness it would have given him additional stature among his family and clan by keeping the property in the family. We know little of either estate, but Ardentinnie appears to have ultimately been given to his nephew, Colin.

Now that he had laid the foundation of his fortune, Great Daniel was about to become embroiled in Scotland's greatest financial disaster, the Darien Scheme, which was to bring the country to its knees financially and precipitate the Act of Union with England.

---

[*] *The Interest of Scotland*, p. 75, William Seton of Pitmedden.
[†] Shawfield MS, No. 233.

'Great' Daniel Campbell of Shawfield and Islay from an etching in Three Generations of Fascinating Women by Constance Russell (the whereabouts of the original is unknown)

2

The Darien Disaster

The Darien Disaster was, in the short term, a catastrophe for Scotland; in the long term it was probably the catalyst that dragged a mainly reluctant country into the Union. The voyages and the affairs of the Company Trading to Africa and the Indies have been well documented. These books make fascinating and, in many ways, shocking reading. Daniel was involved both as a substantial subscriber and as the owner of the ship *Adventure* which suffered an attempted act of piracy by desperate survivors of the first expedition.[*]

The end of the seventeenth century witnessed Scotland in dire poverty. 'North Britain' may have shared a king with England but unfortunately this one had gone to extraordinary lengths to ruin Scotland's trading ventures. The Navigation Acts of 1660 and 1663 had excluded the country from legal trade with any of the English settlements in North America, Africa and the West Indies. After 1660 (the date of the Restoration) Charles II's wars with Holland had also been highly damaging to Scottish trade. The English refused to tolerate competition. They could not have foreseen the expansion and development of the tiny colonies stretching down the eastern seaboard into the prosperous United States of today, instead recognising them as a useful dumping ground for undesirables and criminals,[†] in addition to being a rich source of raw materials such as salt, sugar, tobacco and, of course, the timber that was so vital for the expanding Royal Navy. Exported goods were mainly textiles, the famous salt cured herrings and manufactured goods.

By 1695, at the age of about 25, Daniel had already made a small fortune sufficient to permit him to be one of the largest investors when the subscription books were opened for the Darien Scheme. He subscribed £1,000 to the Company Trading to Africa and the Indies; by comparison his clan chief, Argyll, subscribed £1,500—an irony being that while Daniel could afford it, his Chief almost certainly could not.

This venture was the dream of William Paterson.[‡] A most resourceful Scot, he had spent years in the West Indies where he heard of the 'promised land' on the northern coast of Panama where it was rumoured that the country was

---

[*]   Prebble, *The Darien Disaster*, pp. 229, 230.
[†]   Cromwell had dispatched around 5,000 Scots to New England.
[‡]   Paterson was also principally responsible for the founding of the Bank of England.

lush and fruitful and gold was undoubtedly to be found. The primary source of this report on Darien was a man called Lionel Wafer and the co-directors were mesmerised by his fulsome accounts of 'Paradise'. Nobody questioned why Spain, long established on the Spanish Main, had failed to colonise Darien. Nor did they foresee that the Spaniards might object to the arrival of the Scots. Extravagant optimism carried plans for the expedition forward.

This came at a time when Scotland was badly in need of a bright future after years of misery and poverty. The passage of the Act for the establishment of a trading company by the Scottish Parliament has been described 'as if a window had been opened, flooding the grey and impoverished rooms of Scotland with the sunlight of the Indies ...'.* People rushed to subscribe. The scheme had originally been promoted as a joint English/Scots venture and in June 1695 the Marquis of Tweeddale had touched the Act with the royal sceptre without William III ever having read it.† In doing this, the Marquis, who was not renowned for his intelligence, had failed to meet the legal requirement that any such Act must be approved by the King to ensure that it had received the royal assent; the King had been away in Holland at the time. In November 1695, a subscription book was opened in London; in December, the House of Lords debated the Act and, finding it likely to be highly prejudicial to English trade,‡ presented it to the King. William was furious, declaring himself 'ill served in Scotland'. He dismissed Tweeddale from office.

In January 1696, English subscribers withdrew, leaving Scotland to go it alone. The Scots were quite certain that this was a golden opportunity and the shares were rapidly taken up. In the euphoria of the moment nobody contemplated that Darien might be a totally unsuitable place for such a settlement. Moreover, following a protest by the Spanish Ambassador, William had forbidden all English settlements, colonies and even the Royal Navy from giving any assistance to, or trading with, the Scots under any circumstances. This harsh interdiction was to be responsible for many deaths over the next three years. The Government in London also let it be known that it would look very severely upon any investment made in the scheme by foreign governments. For example, Sir Paul Ricaut, English Resident in Hamburg joined with the English Envoy at His Majesty's Court at Luneburg in a memorial to the Senate in Hamburg threatening them with the 'heighth [sic] of His Majesty's displeasure if they joined with the Scots in any Treaty or Commerce whatsoever.'§

The capital sum subscribed amounted to £419,094 8s 7d and most of it came from Lowlanders. This amount is thought to have represented approximately half the capital of Scotland and underlines the crushing poverty of the nation at that time. Few clan chiefs, other than Argyll, seem to have invested in the

---

* Prebble, *The Darien Disaster.*
† Brown, *History of Scotland*, vol. III.
‡ In particular the East India company.
§ *An Enquiry into the Cause of the Miscarriage of the Scots Colony at Darien or an answer to a Libel*, Glasgow 1700, p. 21.

scheme, probably owing to a shortage of cash. However, MacFarlane of that Ilk subscribed, along with a long list of Campbells, including Daniel and his brother Matthew. The Dowager Duchess of Hamilton was one of the most significant private investors, subscribing £3,000.

Finally, following months of preparation, five ships sailed from the Port of Leith on 14 July 1698. Little or no logical thought had been given to appropriate equipment despite Wafer having told them that '... for about four or six weeks, there will be settled, continued rains of several days and nights' and ''tis a very wet country'.[*] The goods the first expedition carried were about as inappropriate as could be and included 1,500 bibles and 4,000 periwigs.[†]

The first problem arose when it was realised that the ships were woefully inadequately provisioned: food rotted and water was foul. Sickness set in at once, with passengers dying in large numbers of fever or 'flux' during the four month voyage. The Commodore of the fleet was the unpleasant Captain Robert Pennycuik of the *St Andrew*. He did not get on with the equally unpleasant Captain Robert Drummond of the *Caledonia*, a greedy man who, together with his brother, Thomas Drummond, was to be the cause of much misery; both were to survive.

Within days of arrival at Darien, William Paterson's wife had died. Life there was impossible for the ill-equipped Scots and in June 1699 after six months of appalling hardship and great loss of life, it was decided to abandon the settlement. When a Spanish ship entered the bay a few weeks later, the skipper found more than 400 graves. The Reverend Francis Borland, a member of the second expedition and, indeed, the only minister to return home, published an account of his experience in 1715 which corroborates all other descriptions of the Peninsula '... Darien is pernicious, unwholesome and contagious, ... thou devourest men and eatest up thy inhabitants ... what with bad water, salt spoiled provisions, and absence of medicines, the fort was indeed like an hospital of sick and dying men'.[‡]

Finally, on 22 June 1699 the *Endeavour, Caledonia* and *Unicorn* left the Colony to sail to New York. With Captain Pennycuik aboard, the *St Andrew* set sail for Jamaica. Deducing that the Company in Scotland would refuse to pay the men's wages after the great losses incurred by the expedition, Pennycuik decided not to risk returning home but to try his luck as a privateer. Unfortunately for him, he died at sea and his crew, denied any help on arrival at Jamaica, abandoned the ship there. This ship may also have carried Colonel John Campbell of Kilberrie. He had also decided that it would be unwise to return home and set out to establish himself in Jamaica, eventually becoming known as Colonel John Campbell of the Black River.

---

[*] Prebble, *The Darien Disaster.*
[†] Brown, *History of Scotland*, vol. III.
[‡] 'The Darien Scheme', Spencer Collection, University of Glasgow Library, Special Collections.

As for the convoy sailing north to New York, Captain Drummond made it clear that he had no intention of looking after the other two ships, but when the *Endeavour* sank on 1 July, he was forced to put about to pick up survivors; there were too many witnesses.[*] In the event he was probably grateful to have some more seamen on the *Caledonia* as a great number of his own men were now too weak to crew the ship competently.

The *Caledonia* arrived in New York on 4 August but her Captain and crew were to be bitterly disappointed by their reception. England had sent instructions that no aid was to be given to the wretched Caledonians, and they were left sick and virtually starving. Eventually the Governor of New England, Richard Coote, Earl of Bellamont, relented sufficiently to permit the Scots to buy some stores on credit.

Robert Drummond knew both that his ship and few remaining crew members were unfit to put to sea in the Atlantic gales of autumn. So when his brother, Thomas, proposed an act of piracy, he agreed. They decided to seize one of the merchant ships lying in the East River, New York. Their chosen ship was the *Adventure*—property of Daniel Campbell. It has been suggested[†] that because the *Adventure* was a Scottish ship, the Drummonds could maintain that their seizure of her would be legal '… there was some legality in what they proposed, that the Company's Act gave them the power to take, hold and possess any ship of Scotland they desired'.[‡] Of course, the reality of commandeering another ship, even if owned by a Scot, was quite another thing.

The skipper of the *Adventure*, John Howell, had been hired in St Kitts to replace her previous captain who had died there of fever.[§] He had proved extravagant and a rogue according to Daniel's agent in St Kitts, but on this occasion he seems to have acted wisely. The Drummond brothers invited him to dine aboard the *Caledonia*. Plying him with wine, they enquired to which port his ship belonged. When he replied 'Glasgow', Robert Drummond said 'then you belong to us. We seize you and you are our prize.' Howell must have been amazed. A boat was sent across to take the *Adventure* with her Dutch pilot still on board. This man refused at gun point to move the ship alongside the *Caledonia*, so the latter's crew were forced to manoeuvre her themselves. The doughty pilot, Peter Wessel, was put on shore where he immediately reported the attempted piracy to the Deputy Governor. Meanwhile, Howell who had been placed under armed guard on the *Adventure*, eventually gave his word that he would accompany the Drummonds ashore and declare that he had 'willingly surrendered his ship to the Company of Scotland'.[¶] However, once ashore, Howell appealed to John Nanfan, Lieutenant Governor of New England. The Drummonds asserted that it was all a great misunderstanding;

*   Prebble, *Darien Disaster*, pp. 218-22.
†   Prebble, *The Darien Disaster*, pp. 229, 230.
‡   *Ibid.*
§   Shawfield MS, 123r, 122v, 129v.
¶   Prebble, *The Darien Disaster*, p. 236.

they had only taken the *Adventure* because Captain Howell and the Pilot were hopelessly incapacitated by drink. Disbelieving every word, Nanfan was nevertheless unable to persuade the Colony's Attorney to support him and was forced to accept the fiction. This did mean, however, that the Drummonds were unable to maintain their grip on the *Adventure*. Obliged to risk the Atlantic Ocean in the autumn gales, Robert Drummond seems to have come to some sort of accommodation with Howell, as he took some of the *Adventure's* crew with him, presumably to help sail a ship which was dangerously short of able-bodied crew. He finally steered the battered, leaking *Caledonia* safely into the Clyde on 21 November 1699.

Thomas Drummond, still dreaming of a colony in Darien, persuaded two men in New York, Stephen Delancey and Thomas Wenham, who were apparently inspired by the Drummonds' attempt to take the *Adventure*, to advance him money to purchase another ship—*Ann of Caledonia*. Thomas sailed from New York on 20 September 1699 under cover of darkness, heading back to Darien. His departure was then discovered by an enraged Deputy Governor, Nanfan. Realising he had been tricked, Nanfan wrote to his superior, Lord Bellamont 'The Caledonians by and with the assistance of their countrymen, have played us not fair', though he was sufficiently circumspect not to mention the attempted piracy. He received a severe reprimand from Lord Bellamont.

Rumours that all was not well with the Colony had begun to filter through to Scotland by September 1699.[*] In a letter from John Campbell of Deptford to his cousin, James, a London merchant, came the news that while in Jamaica he had heard of the catastrophe of Darien, but added that the rumours could not be true. On 4 October there was, incredibly, still talk of another ship going to Darien. Daniel Mackay wrote to the Duke of Hamilton saying that the Africa Company planned to send Captain Alexander Campbell to Darien in a galley. On 8 October the Earl of Orkney wrote to his brother, the Duke of Hamilton that the bad news must have been fabricated, but the next day, news arrived that the *Caledonia* and the *Unicorn* had arrived in New York 'with the debris of our collonce'.[†] Now there could no longer be any doubt.

Evidently, there was talk of little else in London—and presumably in Scotland, too—and by 11 November there 'seems little doubting of the deserting of Darien'. On 16 November, struggling desperately to survive, the Africa Company offered a 12 per cent discount on all who paid their Candlemas subscription immediately.[‡] It would seem unlikely that many took up this offer.

On 6 January 1700 an anonymous note written to the Duke of Hamilton expressed no surprise that the Africa Company failed: 'you have chosen such villains to employ abroad and grosly betrayed at home'.[§]

---

[*] GD406/1/4463, John Campbell, of Deptford, to cousin James Campbell.
[†] GD406/1/4477.
[‡] GD406/1/6947.
[§] GD406/1/4476.

On 10 February Lord Basil Hamilton wrote to his brother (as was frequently the case in their personal correspondence, it was mainly in cipher) giving details of the address in the Lords disapproving of the Scottish settlement in Darien, and describing their decision to propose union in a separate address as a 'fine shugar plum, indeed'.[*]

Upon his arrival in Glasgow, Robert Drummond learned that a second expedition had sailed for Darien on 12 May[†] despite news of the calamitous fate of the first expedition having been received in Scotland months before. Moreover, a third doomed flotilla had left on the 24th of that month—this was despite receiving an urgent message from the Directors telling the Captains to wait. In their haste to leave before the Directors could stop them and determined to make their fortunes, these ships left behind several men and much in the way of stores. Not surprisingly, the second and third expeditions fared no better than the first.

The failure of the Darien Scheme was a hammer blow to Scottish independence and was to prove a major contributory factor in the successful Union seven years later. Scotland was devastated by this blow not only financially but also in terms of national pride. The Scots, not without cause, were quick to blame England and a king who they felt was uninterested in the affairs of his northern kingdom, regarding it merely as a good source of Highland soldiers for his army in the wars against France.

Scotland sent Lord Basil Hamilton, brother of the Duke of Hamilton, to London to ask for help; Lord Carmichael wrote to the Duke saying that the King refused to see Lord Basil despite many requests from prominent personages. William only went so far as to express his sorrow at the disaster and his willingness to support Parliament in any moves to help the Company for Africa and the Indies to make good its losses. William III died shortly afterwards leaving as one of his dying wishes that 'in the interests of both Kingdoms, an incorporating Union should be consummated at the earliest[‡] possible date'. One of the results of Union would be the payment of 'The Equivalent' to Scotland in recompense for the Darien losses (see chapter 5).

Daniel Campbell probably felt he had got off lightly. Not only did he still have his ship, but he was to become a Commissioner for the Equivalent, which in turn ensured that he received the return of his investment of £1,000. He was also shortly to be a Scottish signatory to the Act of Union.

---

[*]   GD406/1/7281.
[†]   There is some confusion over dates here. Brown says the second expedition left on 12 May. This was probably otherwise recorded as a 'relief expedition'.
[‡]   Brown, History of Scotland, vol. III, p. 77.

3

Consolidating a Fortune; Collector of Customs

When Daniel returned to Glasgow in 1694, he was still a young man, about 24 years of age. Having already laid the foundations of a fortune, he immediately began to broaden the range of his business activities—his investment in the Darien Scheme was only one of them. In 1696, the fledgling Bank of Scotland opened a branch in Glasgow which failed.[*] This was largely due to merchants such as Daniel, who functioned as a sort of one-man private bank. Cash was to be in very short supply for many years, especially following the Darien Disaster. Comparable to circumstances today, the most generally accepted security against cash advanced was land. Amongst those people to whom Daniel lent money can be found the names of highand chieftains such as MacAlister of Loup, Stewart of Appin, together with the Montgomeries, Lauderdale, the Duke of Argyll and his brother Ilay, the Earl of Kilmarnock and many others.

Having been appointed burgess in Glasgow in 1694, Daniel's election, some years later, as burgess in Dumbarton in 1703 and in Edinburgh in 1706 was in the nature of being given the freedom of those cities—an honorary position bestowed on prominent figures. It was obvious that he had to receive his appointment in Glasgow since all merchants were required to be burgesses of the town from which they traded and you could not carry on a trade or craft without having achieved this status. Nobody was eligible to be appointed until the Dean of Guild had examined their training, financial worth and moral reputation.[†] A merchant had to show himself to be worth £100 Scots and demonstrate that his name was on the apprentice books of the burgh. Having fulfilled these requirements, a fee was paid and the status of burgess was conferred, giving the right to trade as a merchant. Most of these men only traded within Scotland, or at the very outside in a small way south of the border; others traded solely with Ireland. It was the relatively few true mariner merchants, such as Daniel and Matthew, who set out for the Baltic ports, Spain and the Settlements in America. Many of the burgesses were the younger sons of lairds who needed to make their own way in the world.

---

[*] After two failed attempts to establish a branch in Glasgow, the bank finally opened permanently in 1787.

[†] Smout, *Scottish Historical Review*, vol. 6, p. 58.

Daniel was both well connected and well placed for advancement, thanks to his relationship with Argyll, his Clan Chief, who was himself to benefit from the frequent 'loans' that Daniel supplied.* The 1st Duke was to die in the arms of his mistress in 1703. A great scandal at the time, the Duke's will had conveyed all his property to this woman, a Mrs Peggy Alison. Well-publicised mud-slinging ensued. The Ecclesiastical Court pronouncement was that the Duke 'was said to be basely principled both as to the Church, his King and Country, which made his exit the more acceptable to all honest men'. He had been long estranged from his Duchess, who refused to pay for the funeral and Daniel consequently footed the bill.[†] In any event, despite this potentially embarrassing situation, Daniel continued to have a close relationship with John Campbell, the 2nd Duke.[‡]

In March 1701, Daniel was appointed Collector of Customs at Port Glasgow; an interesting and potentially very profitable position. Given the illegal trade that Daniel had plied between the Americas and Scotland, it is surprising that he was given such a high profile role. Perhaps the appointment had an element of 'poacher turned gamekeeper' about it, turning his expertise and knowledge of the smugglers' techniques to the Government's advantage; it was certainly advantageous to him. His appointment, once again, was due to the influence of his patron, the Duke of Argyll, who would have undoubtedly wanted one of his own men in such a position; the Duke presumably also looked forward to some good brandy that had not had an exorbitant level of duty paid on it.

Daniel's rights and responsibilities to Her Majesty are laid out in a document in the usual pompous official terms.[§] John Leckie of Newlands (presumably his father-in-law) and John Campbell, merchant of Edinburgh (probably his elder brother) were 'Cautions' for Daniel's probity in declaring and paying over all dues and 'just count reckoning and pay to the mannagers of Her Majesty's Customs of all and whatsoever sumes of money as shall intromitted with and by me by virtue of on Account of foreigne Excise or Bullione from Ceasures ... etc etc'. The Collectors, or, as they were often considered, tax farmers, were extremely unpopular and both they and their subordinates were often subjected to harassment and even death. The system was complicated; it appears that the Government anticipated a certain level of revenue and that anything in excess was often kept by the Collector and/ or his subordinate but although this was 'understood', it was also, of course,

---

* The first duke whose funeral Daniel paid for, died in 1703 but he continued the close connection by lending to the 2nd Duke.
† Shawfield MS, no number. Funeral cost £1,620 16s 0d.
‡ In the Argyll papers (T. Stevenson) there is a neat reference to this man. 'He was made Commissioner to Parliament, 6th March 1705. He brought along a certain instrument called a Quondam, which occasioned the debauchery of a great number of ladies of qualitie and other young gentlewoman'. Could this be the first mention of this item?
§ Shawfield MS, 254r.

totally illegal. Daniel's management was to come under close Government scrutiny a few years later when he was accused of corruption.[*]

According to David Stevenson, 'smuggling was Scotland's biggest and most profitable service industry'.[†] In his book, the *Scottish Smuggler*, Gavin Smith writes that Article VI of the Act of Union must have especially displeased the Scots, stating that 'all parts of the United Kingdom from ever from and after the Union shall have the same Allowances, Encouragements and Drawbacks, and be under the same Prohibitions, Restrictions and Regulations of Trade and liable to the same Customs and Duties on Export and Import'.[‡] Despite several exemptions giving Scotland seven years freedom from duty on items such as salt (owing to the fact that the country used a great quantity of salt in the curing of fish, much of which was subsequently re-exported), the Scots were furious. The taxes made many items considerably more expensive, putting them out of reach of a large number of people. The result was a boom in smuggling. People in every walk of life engaged in evading customs dues on items such as wine, tobacco, tea, silks and sugar and Scottish smugglers concentrated on importing goods that were liable for the heaviest duty. Jacobite supporters were seemingly amongst the most prominent of the smugglers but it would appear that almost everyone within reach of the coast, had a finger in the pie.

The Calendar of Treasury Papers for 10 April 1708 has a note:

> various hogsheads of brandy had been picked up on the coast, probably tossed out of the French fleet, thought to be part of a vast quantity of other things that the enemy lost. If this were true it was an undoubted proof of their having been under a most horrid consternation, and that they had already found themselves great losers for undertaking their late expedition. It would discourage them for ever from attempting the like.

A somewhat optimistic view, one would think with hindsight. The minute continues by indicating that the brandy must have been recuperated by people who had avoided the payment of any excise duty and that it was plain the Queen had been greatly defrauded. It lays the blame on 'vice-admirals of the coast and lords of the manor' for introducing prohibited goods, commenting that '[clearly] if the casks of brandy are made strong enough to resist beating on "mustle banks etc,." the brandy takes no harm'. Daniel was undoubtedly aware and probably personally involved in all of this since he was the Collector (see page 29).

Daniel did not hold the position of Collector for the Port of Glasgow beyond 1708 but there are some other interesting and detailed accounts of his rather dubious activities whilst in that post. For example, at the end of

---

[*] Calendar of Treasury Papers, vol. CVI, p. 26 in The National Archives.
[†] Stevenson, *The Beggar's Benison*.
[‡] Smith, *The Scottish Smuggler*.

May 1707, immediately after the Act of Union had been put into effect, Boyer records a Transaction relating to the Customs in Scotland, 'whereby her Majesty hath been considerably defrauded':

> In the latter end of May, 1707, the Three following Ships, (viz.) the Neptune of Glasgow, the *Eagle Galley*, and the *May Flower* of Glasgow, arrived in the Road of Greenock loaded with Brandy from France; and the ship called the Recovery of Douwart, arrived likewise about the same time on the west coast of Scotland; but no Entry was made, or Customs paid, for any Goods on board the said Ships though it appears that the same Goods were landed in Scotland. But the Fact will be most fairly stated and best understood by reciting the substance of some of the Depositions taken on this Occasion.[*]

The tricks that were played and the part that some of the officials, in this case Daniel, took in these illegal enterprises are further elaborated:

> Archibald Maclean, Tide-Water [waiter] at Port Glasgow, deposed that he and another Waiter were sent by John Kaltfor [Kaltsoe], Surveyor of the said Port, on board the *Eagle*, which he saw loaded with Brandy; That he was likewise on Board the *Neptune* and *May Flower*, which were then unladed, but was told by the Waiters on board that they had likewise been loaded with Brandy; that the said Deponent was ordered by Kaltsoe, a Surveyor, to continue on board the *Eagle*, until she arrived at the Isle of Man,[†] or some part of Ireland; that as soon as this ship was under Sail, she began to unlade into several Lighters which came to her Side for that Purpose; and that the Deponent and the other Waiter were shut up, and kept in the Cabin during the Time of their unlading.

William Semple and James Ronald deposed,

> that being Waiters at Port Glasgow, they were sent on board the *Neptune* by John Kaltsoe, Surveyor, and were told by the Sailors that she was loaded with Brandy from France; that they were threatened and commanded by the Master and ship's crew to betake themselves to the Cabin, where they were shut up and kept during the Time the Goods were unloaded.

Semple further deposed 'that while he was on board the Neptune, he saw several small boats about the *May Flower* and *Eagle Galley*'. Thomas Kennedy, Land Waiter (customs officer based on the shore) at Port Glasgow, deposed that he saw several of the lighters which transported the brandy from the *Eagle*, *Neptune* and the *May Flower* 'in their course from the said Ships and coming into the key of Port Glasgow ...'.

There were many more depositions, including several stating that the people involved had seen blank permits in the Cabin signed by Daniel

---

[*] Boyer, *Political State*, vol. VII, pp. 373, 374.

[†] The Isle of Man was a haven for smuggling, lying as it does between Scotland and Ireland.

Campbell. The witnesses also reported that when they had come ashore, their superior officer had not demanded any account of them, which left them feeling that the man must be conniving in what had happened with respect to the *Neptune* and the *Eagle Galley*. The three witnesses were then dismissed from their jobs. They applied to Daniel for some compensation and were referred to Richard Murray who served as Daniel's Secretary in the Customs Office. Murray gave them ten pounds over and above their salaries—a considerable sum. After their subsequent depositions giving information against Daniel, Murray told them to repay the money!*

Other witnesses also made statements. One Robert Noble, Tidesman at Glasgow, said that he knew the greater part of the *Neptune* and all of her cargo belonged to Daniel and his partners. A quantity of evidence was given and there can be small room for doubt that Daniel was making a huge profit. On the occasion referred to above, the four ships were quickly sent away to lie off the Isle of Bute in order to avoid being taken by the Government when Sir Robert Dixon arrived to inquire into the incident. Daniel's cousin, Dugald Campbell, who was skipper of the *Neptune*, received a letter from Daniel telling him to put all tide waiter employees ashore and to set sail immediately. Thomas Smith, a Glasgow merchant and Daniel's partner, had been supervising the unloading of the ships in Port Glasgow. He was questioned under oath, but 'refused to give any satisfaction, and said he did not apprehend himself obliged to answer such questions'.†

Daniel, himself, was then examined. He 'swore he knew nothing of any goods landed out of them [the *Neptune* and the *Eagle Galley*] in any Port either in North Britain or South Britain'.‡ On being further interrogated, he 'declined answering so particular a Question'. The Commission of Enquiry did not presume to offer any other Remarks on this Fact, other than, 'That if we suppose the ships to be fully loaded, as it is most probably they were, the quantity of brandy would amount to Three hundred and forty ton' that if it had been seized, the Duties (as French brandy) would have amounted to 'twenty eight thousand one hundred and eighty six pounds or therabouts': an enormous sum. Daniel did not function on a small scale!

The matter was raised in the House of Commons on 10 April§ where the following is entered:

> Enclosed is a letter from Mr. John Campbell,¶ the Parliament man, and uncle to the Duke of Argyle, that it be read to the Lord High Treasurer. It would demonstrate that must become of them, for all this bluster upon Sir Robert [Dixon] and the Board was because Mr. Daniel Campbell had

---

* Boyer, *Political State*, vol. VII, p. 374.
† Boyer, *Political State*, vol. VII, p. 376.
‡ *Ibid.*
§ *Calendar of Treasury Papers, 1708-1714*, vol. CVI, pp. 26, 27.
¶ John Campbell of Mamore.

access to the Duke and his uncle ... His ambition was to restore the two Campbells (see above) whom they passed over at Port Glasgow, where he was collector, because they had shunned Sir Robert when he went to inquire respecting four ships that ran brandies ... they hoped that Mr. Daniel Campbell would be brought to account for tho' he had not performed his duty, he ought not to molest those that had ...

The influence of Argyll in Glasgow was such that poor Sir Robert was heavily leaned on to restore the two Campbells to their jobs as tide waiters and to accept that Daniel 'has done you justice in his representations and wee are both confounded at the hardship is done to any of the name of Campbell since none have appeared more ready to serve the Queen was wee'.

The House well understood that Her Majesty had been significantly defrauded; but, after considerable debate, took no action. One can only imagine that this was not an isolated case. The affair trickled on for some time, but Daniel managed to avoid more than the mildest censure, although it is clear that he was guilty. His behaviour in this matter is very likely the reason why he was not returned as Member for Glasgow in the election in June of the same year. Instead the Provost of Glasgow, Robert Rodgers, was elected. Daniel was obviously extremely disappointed and

> laid a project of disappointing the legal election by a sham election of himself, combining with Collin Campbell for that purpose. Mr. Campbell's procedure was absolutely null, because by the Acts of Parliament the common clerk of the presiding burgh was the only person empowered to make a return ... If Mr. Campbell did not desist, it was expected that he would be exemplarily punished.[*]

In September 1707, it is recorded in Treasury Papers 'last week we sent to Mr. Campbell, late Collector of Port Glasgow, who coming to us after making many frivolous excuses for delay, dictated a report [unfortunately this is missing] which was hoped would show how far he has dealt sincerely or not'.[†]

One interesting comment on these events is that, at the time, the retiring Customs Commissioners would burn all their records. Only in December 1716 did an order go out that all such records should be delivered to their successors. This is, of course, why so many of the early Scottish Customs Records are missing.

---

[*] Calendar of Treasury Papers, vol. CVII, p. 41.
[†] Treasury Book V, XXI, part II, p. 429.

4

Daniel in Politics

There were at least two principal reasons for Daniel seeking election to Parliament. The first, and most important, was that the Duke of Argyll needed his men in positions where they could further his own ends. Secondly, to be elected to Parliament, by whatever means, was to demonstrate that you were a man of substance and standing in the community. The late seventeenth and early eighteenth centuries represented a period when only a candidate with support—often financial, but also political—from local magnates, could expect to gain a seat.

As a member of the most powerful Clan in Scotland, a prosperous merchant in his own right and an active citizen of Glasgow, Daniel Campbell was an ideal candidate to be proposed by the 1st Duke of Argyll as Commissioner for Inveraray in 1702.[*] Moreover, his election to this, the last Scottish Parliament before Union, seems to have been one of the few contests of his political career to be devoid of controversy! He sat in the Scottish Parliament from 1702 until it was abolished following Union in 1707. Naturally, he followed the voting path of his patron, by then John, 2nd Duke of Argyll.

So much has been written about the Union, the pros, the cons, the opposers and the supporters, that this chapter only proposes to deal with events in so far as they involved the Great Daniel. In 2007, when some are celebrating the 300th anniversary of the successful conclusion to the Treaty negotiations that gave such a boost to Scottish trade and development, it is ironic that many Scots are again wondering whether they might not do better on their own.

Scotland's affairs were certainly in a catastrophic condition at the end of the seventeenth century. Efforts to pacify the Highlands and root out the Jacobites had led to the massacre of Glencoe in 1692, a calculated and terrible act directly ordered by King William and one for which he evidently felt no remorse.[†] Instead, the blame for the massacre, as generally and erroneously represented in history, was conveniently set squarely on the shoulders of the Clan Campbell.

---

[*]   Young, *The Parliaments of Scotland*, vol. 1. Scottish Archive Press.

[†]   'As for the McDonalds of Glencoe, if they can be well distinguished from the rest of the Highlanders, it will be proper, for the vindication of public justice, to extirpate that set of thieves. W.R.'

The failure of the Darien Scheme, had encouraged the English to raise, once again, the question of an incorporating Union with the northern Kingdom. The first serious attempt to achieve this came in late 1702, some six months after the death of King William who had long cherished the idea of a full incorporating Union. It was a failure. On this occasion, shocked by the failure of the Company Trading to Africa and the effects of failed harvests leading to literal starvation for many, Scotland was possibly more ready to treat than her southern neighbour but with the English failing to produce a quorum eight times during the discussions, the effort was abandoned.

The following year the issue of Union was approached once again. England was now the suitor, Scotland the reluctant bride, but both had their reasons for wanting it. The Scots preferred a federal union (if, indeed, they wanted one at all) and were desperate to be able to trade freely and legally with the rest of the world, including the English colonies, while maintaining their own authority over Kirk and the Law. In addition, there was a very real threat that England might invade to force a union, which would have certainly imposed burdens on the Kingdom of North Britain. For their part, the English wished to prevent further trouble from alliances the Scots might make with the old enemy, France, and were also eager to ensure the Protestant/Hanoverian succession. For this purpose, the Act of Settlement had been written into law by the English Parliament in London in 1701. This Act had settled the Protestant Succession on Sophia, Electress of Hanover, in the anticipated event that Anne, who would succeed her sister and brother-in-law William, would also die leaving no surviving heir.* Sophia's position as the nearest eligible successor in the royal line, stems from her descent as the granddaughter of James I of England (James VI of Scotland) and, accordingly, sister to Charles II. The Act restricted the throne (English at that time) to the Protestant heirs of Sophia of Hanover, who had never embraced the Catholic faith nor married a Roman Catholic. (In the event, Sophia died just before Queen Anne in June 1714, and her son, George Ludwig of Hanover, succeeded in her place.)

The Scottish Parliament retaliated with the Act of Security which guaranteed Scotland the right to choose its own monarch after the death of Queen Anne. Highly irritated by this bravado on the part of the Scots, the English introduced the Alien Act in 1705. This classified all Scots as 'aliens' until the succession should be clarified:

> ... no person or Persons being a native or Natives of the Kingdom of Scotland shall be capable to inherit any Lands, Tenements or Hereditaments within this Kingdom of England ... or to enjoy any Benefit or Advantage of a natural born Subject of England: But every such Person shall be from henceforth adjudged and taken as an Alien.

---

* Queen Anne endured a large number of pregnancies (eighteen?) but only one child survived to the age of ten.

The irate Scots refused to discuss any form of union until the Act was rescinded. Its implementation would be yet another devastating political blow to a Scottish economy already undermined both by the fiasco of Darien and the catastrophe of famine following the failure of harvests in the years 1695-9 (together often referred to as the seven bad years). It would also have been a severe shock to some influential Scots—mainly peers—who owned handsome properties in England and enjoyed preference at Court. In November 1705, the House of Lords voted that it should be repealed.

The writer Daniel Defoe was a keen observer of the events that were leading slowly but inexorably towards a Union. He not only published his *Review* but served as a sort of spy for Robert Harley, Secretary of State for England. Defoe was poorly regarded by the Scots, who thought him dishonest; he, in turn, labelled them 'a hardened, refractory and terrible people'.[*]

Scott describes the 'critical problem of the relationship with England. It was a struggle that fell into two phases: a period of determination to assert Scottish independence from May 1703 to September 1705, and the collapse of that resistance, leading to the eventual approval of the Treaty in January 1707'.[†] This period was indeed a dour struggle.

In Scotland, the pro-Union faction was led by the Earl of Mar, a clever man who worked very hard for an integrated Union. Unfortunately, after 1707, he became rapidly disenchanted and changed his coat, professing to regret his action in supporting the Union. It also transpired that while expressing enthusiasm for the Hanoverian succession, he had been in constant contact with the Pretender.[‡] He was not alone in keeping a foot in both camps; a fact of which first King William and then Queen Anne were well aware. Feeling himself to have been snubbed by King George, Mar eventually turned to the Jacobites, raising the Pretender's standard in rebellion at Braemar on 6 March 1715, proclaiming him King of Scotland and Great Britain and Ireland (see page 43).

A total of five Scottish dukes played prominent roles in the run up towards Union: Argyll, Queensberry, Montrose, Hamilton and Atholl. These proud nobles engaged in an extraordinary level of double-dealing and conspiracy. Riley writes

> the Scottish magnates and their followers, whether in or out, were completely devoid of any sense of responsibility for anything but their own prospects ... The Government was looked upon as an institution to be exploited. Without qualms the greater nobles would undertake to carry a policy they had no affection for and knowing it had no hope of success. At least it gave them an office and a salary ...[§]

---

*   *The Political and Economic Writings of Daniel Defoe: Union with Scotland*, vol. 4.

†   Scott, *The Union of Scotland and England*, vol.iii, pp. 159, 160.

‡   Brown, *History of Scotland*, vol. III.

§   *The Union of 1707*, ed. Rae, p. 7.

In a letter written by the Earl of Roxburghe to George Baillie of Jerviswood, he succinctly covers the reasons for swaying the votes:

> The motive will be Trade with most, Hanover with some, ease and security with others together with a generall aversion at civill discords, intolerable poverty and the constant oppression of a bad ministry from generation to generation, without the least regard to the good of the Country ...[*]

Three parties emerged: the Court Party with Argyll, Mar, Montrose and their followers; the Country Party, otherwise known as the 'Squadrone', led by the erratic and debt-laden Duke of Hamilton together with Roxburghe, Tweeddale and Andrew Fletcher of Saltoun at its head; and the Jacobites or Cavalier Party led by the Earl of Home, which differed little from the Country party in most respects, but were insistent on the return of the Stewart monarchy. Fletcher, a well-known opponent of any form of Union, wrote: 'Scotland was totally neglected like a farm managed by servants and not under the eye of the master'.[†] By the time that Treaty negotiations began, the majority of the 'Squadrone' had more or less accepted that an incorporating Union was probably going to be both the most likely and, in the long term, the best result for Scotland. They finally conceded that Scottish trade was going to benefit (and Roxburghe eventually received a Dukedom in recognition of swapping sides).

George Lockhart of Carnwarth, a prominent Jacobite, was fiercely anti-union, although, to his own expressed astonishment, he was appointed as a Commissioner to negotiate for the Treaty of Union. He was to be the sole Scottish Commissioner to vote against Union and he refused to put his signature to the Act. He despised Daniel Campbell, whom he described as an arrogant, grasping fellow. Both were patriotic Scotsmen but they were poles apart in their philosophy. When Lockhart referred to the bestowal of Collectorships of the Customs as a common form of bribery during the run up to Union,[‡] one can well imagine that he had Daniel in mind.

By this time, Daniel was Commissioner for Inveraray and therefore in the pocket of the Duke of Argyll. He duly followed the Argathelian line and was eventually appointed a Commissioner to treat for the Union, when the Scottish Parliament agreed to open negotiations for a treaty with England in September 1705. It was decided that the Queen should be asked to nominate the Commission as opposed to the appointments being made by Parliament. This was a somewhat surprising suggestion coming, as it did, from the erratic Duke of Hamilton, who was fiercely anti-union at that time; everyone knew that the Queen's selection was, without doubt, likely to appoint pro-Union commissioners. Was George Lockhart named as a token sop to the antis? He

---

[*] Jerviswood Correspondence, p. 138.
[†] Fletcher, *Political Works*, 1749.
[‡] Fletcher of Saltoun, *Political Works*, p. 255.

foresaw the incorporating Union desired by England as likely to 'rivet the Scots in perpetual slavery' to their southern neighbours.

There were 31 Scottish Commissioners including Daniel Campbell, a representative of the Burghs and one of the few members not of the nobility. Neither the Duke of Argyll nor the Duke of Hamilton were nominated as members of the Commission, but in other respects it was primarily composed of members of the Government. Hamilton was evidently disappointed not to be appointed but Argyll was well occupied serving in Marlborough's Army on the continent. The rest of the Commissioners were a curious mixture, as it was necessary to select 31 theoretically representative Scots of sufficient stature, who would be prepared to work towards a common result—not at all an easy task![*] When the Squadrone came out in favour of Union, the Duke of Hamilton wrote to his mother 'my heart is broke'.[†]

The representatives were as follows: the Duke of Queensberry, the Earl of Seafield, Earl of Mar, Earl of Loudon, Earl of Sutherland, Earl of Wemyss, Earl of Morton, Earl of Leven, Earl of Stair, Earl of Rosebery, Earl of Glasgow, Lord Archibald Campbell (brother to the Duke of Argyll), Viscount Duplin, Lord Ross, Sir Hugh Dalrymple, Adam Cockburn of Ormiston, Sir Robert Dundas of Arniston, Robert Steuart of Tillicoulty, Francis Montgomery, Sir David Dalrymple, Sir Alexander Ogilvie of Forglen, Sir Patrick Johnston (Lord Provost of Edinburgh), Sir James Smollett of Bonhill, Alexander Grant of that Ilk, William Seton Jr of Pitmedden, George Lockhart of Carnwath, William Morrison of Prestongrange, John Clerk, Jr of Pencuik, Hugh Montgomery (formerly Provost of Glasgow), Daniel Stewart and Daniel Campbell of Ardentinny.

The first meeting of the two sides took place in the Cockpit at Whitehall in London in April 1706. The Scottish commissioners took care to ensure that the results of their deliberations did not become public knowledge back home north of the border during the negotiations.[‡] This added fuel to the flames of the anti-unionists in Scotland who were convinced that they were being sold out. Also it seems that certain commissioners, such as Lockhart, were excluded from some of the discussions; in other words there were inner cabals or committees to thrash out specific articles.[§] Where Daniel Campbell stood in this it is impossible to know with any certainty but he was probably included in discussions on subjects on which he was best informed: trade and excise.[¶] Since many articles would have had direct bearing on Daniel's own activities, including all those relating to excise, duties and the ownership of

---

[*] Brown, *History of Scotland*, vol. III, p. 102.
[†] GD406/1/7921 and 7146.
[‡] Whatley proposes that these rumours were deliberately circulated by the Presbyterian churchmen.
[§] Lockhart asserted that he took no part but merely served as an observer.
[¶] Whatley, *The Scots and Union*, p. 236.

shipping, it is likely that he was busy.[*] The two sets of commissioners, English and Scottish, sat separately in London and, following prolonged negotiation, agreed the Treaty. During the negotiations the two sides rarely met, apart from in the Cockpit. They apparently communicated almost entirely by written messages. The only recorded meeting between both sides in the course of negotiation was when they discussed the question of the number of Scottish representatives that were to sit at Westminster.[†] Evidently, they did not socialise either.[‡] They did, however, congregate in the great hall of the Cockpit on three ceremonial occasions in the presence of the Queen: upon her address before deliberations were begun, halfway when she enquired about progress and finally when all had been agreed.

Once the details of the Act had been hammered out, both sides returned to their respective Parliaments for official ratification of the Articles. Events moved rather swifter in the Scottish Parliament than in the English Parliament, due to the fact, according to Sir Walter Scott,[§] that nobility, barons and burgesses 'a' sate thegither, cheek by jowl and then they didna need to have the same blethers twice over'—a description appropriate to many parliaments today. The Scottish Parliament worked through the treaty article by article from October 1706 until the following January. Mar described it as very hard work and recorded that they often laboured all day with no pause even for refreshment. Each article had to be debated and voted on in turn. Members of the Parliament who had not served as commissioners needed to be cajoled and bribed. Those who indicated that they would remain firmly opposed to Union, were told that they could expect no further favour at Court.

Meanwhile, opposition was consolidating throughout Scotland. Troops had to be deployed to maintain order in several major towns and cities, including Edinburgh and Glasgow. One of the biggest concerns amongst the people was the new burden of taxation that was likely to fall on an already weak economy. The level of taxation in both countries was ultimately intended to be uniform, but at the time, taxation in England was higher. As a result, concessions were to be granted to the Scots in several areas, including on the vital commodities of malt and salt.[¶] In order to promote the Scottish herring fishing, duty paid on salt could be clawed back from the Government. It gave smugglers a great opportunity to bring in illegal salt to be used in pickling the fish and then to claim back duty which had not been paid in the first instance. Also the salt brought in from Ireland was of a higher quality than that which was farmed in the Firth of Forth, adding to the Excise Officers'

---

[*]   Article v (ownership of ships), vii, (liquor) viii (salt), xv (equality of trade/equivalent) for example.

[†]   Papers of Sir John Clerk of Penicuik.

[‡]   Mar and Kellie Papers, 3 August 1706, states: 'None of the English during the Treaty had one of the Scots so much as to dine or drink a glass of wine with them'.

[§]   Scott, *Rob Roy*.

[¶]   *The Scottish Parliament and the Union of 1707*, NAS pamphlet.

problems. Herring was caught in such numbers at that time that the Glasgow magistrates would often send barrels of salted fish as gifts to influential persons in London and Edinburgh.[*]

Pamphleteers were busy, principally on the opposition side. One of the best known of these men, James Hodges, was dismissive of an incorporating Union writing that the Scotland was the most ancient kingdom in Europe and, in short, pronouncing that she was infinitely superior to England. He had no truck with the financial arguments saying that the Scots would be foolish to barter their independence for 'some hogsheads of sugar, indigo and stinking tobacco of the Plantation trade'. Daniel Campbell, for whom these items were his bread and butter, could not have agreed with any of this!

Of the 25 articles of the Act of Union, the one which created the most furore was that which stipulated that there were only going to be 45 Scottish members to represent 'North Britain' in the Parliament in London. The English had 513, which was out of all proportion despite the much larger population in the south.[†]

The major sop to Scottish opinion and pride was the strangely designated 'Equivalent'. The sum of £398,085 10s was to be paid to Scotland to compensate for taking on a share of England's national debt, to repay those shareholders who had lost their investment in the Darien Disaster and to pay arrears of salaries to government officials and the army. Daniel had been one of the larger investors in the Darien Scheme and, in view of his position, it is likely he was amongst the fortunate ones to receive compensation.[‡]

The Articles were finally approved by the Scottish Parliament on 16 January 1707. The Act was carried by 110 in favour and 67 against. The English Parliament also voted in favour of the Act which finally received the Royal Assent on 6 March, 1707; it was finally signed, sealed and delivered and came into effect on 1 May. There was certainly no majority of opinion in favour in Scotland and the Act was pushed through mainly by the efforts of the nobility. Cynically, one might say that a few acted from principle but most had only an eye for the main chance—their own advancement. It had taken a great deal of negotiation and much bribery; Lockhart was incensed at the 'secret' payment of £22,000 made to the Duke of Queensberry. The monies were paid through Sir James Gray to avoid the obvious appearance of bribery, but was for the Duke to dispense as he thought best. It is hard to see it as anything other than 'palm greasing'. The Duke is thought to have kept something approaching £12,000 for himself and he also received a further payment of £14,575 in 1707. Much of this was to defray his allowances and expenses incurred over the Treaty negotiations.[§] The Commissioners, who

---

[*] MacArthur, *History of the Port of Glasgow*.

[†] Article xxii. England is estimated to have had a population of roughly five million and Scotland one million in the early years of the eighteenth century.

[‡] In the form of debentures.

[§] Archives of the RBS.

had journeyed to London throughout the haggling, were all given 'expenses'; although the nobles received more,[*] generally speaking twice as much, than the few lesser fry, such as Daniel. The cost of a journey to London and six months lodging there was estimated at a cost of £500—a very significant sum at the time.[†] Robbie Burns' oft quoted line 'We're bought and sold for English gold, Such a parcel of rogues in a nation' was pretty apt.

This was also the moment when Daniel suddenly received his compensation of £700 from the Admiralty for the ships he had lost to the French some eleven years earlier; despite being awarded the money in 1696, he had never received the payment. English negotiators for the Union were evidently taking no risks where Scottish Commissioners were concerned.

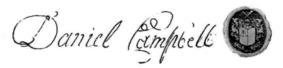

Daniel's signature appears on the Act of Union, elegantly drawn beside his seal of crossed oars.[‡] (His handwriting was certainly better than most of the other signatories.) It must have been a momentous day for the pro-Unionist minority, but there were many who were crushed by despair; these included Andrew Fletcher of Saltoun, Lockhart, the Duke of Hamilton and Lord Belhaven. Fletcher was a true patriot and perhaps, at heart, a republican. Following the passing of the Act of Union he forsook politics. Lockhart continued to be active in Jacobite affairs and was probably fortunate to have escaped a charge of treason. His brother, Philip, was executed as a traitor when the 'rebels' surrendered after the Battle of Preston in November 1715. Many years later, in 1727, Lockhart learned that he was on the point of arrest for his contact with the then exiled Mar, who had been accused of High Treason following the events of the '15. Lockhart escaped to Rotterdam. He was subsequently told that he might return home to Scotland but that he must pass by way of London. He tried to avoid this but it was made a condition of his return. He duly arrived in London and Sir Robert Walpole insisted that he be introduced to King George II. Unwillingly, Lockhart agreed and further promised that he would withdraw from public life and live quietly at home. He had finally come to accept that there was no chance of success for the Stewarts.[§]

The fragility of the Union soon became apparent. Taking advantage of discontent, there was a potentially serious Jacobite rebellion in 1708, when a French invasion fleet sailed into the Moray Firth, and in 1713 a motion in the House to overthrow the Union was narrowly defeated by only four votes.

---

* £1,000 each.
† 'Essay upon the Union etc.' (Edinburgh 1706), p. 29.
‡ The crossed oars of Skipness.
§ Lockhart Register of Letters, pp. 132-3 and 396.

Although it took many years before the benefits of Union could be felt in Scotland, it was surely of instant help to merchants such as Daniel, since it removed all the barriers to trade that had been imposed by the English. For the majority of ordinary Scots, however, it would be at least a further generation before they really began to thrive.

Daniel was one of the original 43 Scottish members to sit at Westminster, but he was not re-elected in 1708, much to his disgust. There were two returns made for this contest. The constituency of Glasgow Burghs was made up of Glasgow, Rutherglen, Renfrew and Dumbarton; the burghs frequently had different patrons and at each election a different Burgh had the right of being the 'returning' burgh which had a casting vote. Daniel had the support of Renfrew; his opposition, Provost Robert Rodgers was supported by Dumbarton. Failing to be elected principally thanks to the Duke of Montrose's support for Rodgers—'anything to keep a Campbell out"—Daniel appealed but his apparently high-handed behaviour ruined any prospect of compromise and the Provost was duly confirmed as the legitimate member. Daniel was extremely displeased and

> laid a project of disappointing the legal election by a sham election of himself, combining with Collin Campbell for that purpose. Mr. Campbell's procedure was absolutely null, because by the Acts of Parliament the common clerk of the presiding burgh was the only person empowered to make a return ... If Mr. Campbell did not desist, it was expected that he would be exemplarily punished.[†]

They may not have agreed on many things but both the Duke of Hamilton and the Duke of Montrose loathed Daniel, and had avowed desires to keep him out of Parliament. This is interesting because many of the records telling us of this are from 1705/6 when he had not yet made an obvious mark in public life, so far as one can tell, although the two Dukes would naturally have been opposed to his advancement thanks to his Argyll connection. Correspondence in the Hamilton manuscript relates how the Hamiltons were incensed by Daniel's purchase of his first major piece of property, Shawfield, on the banks of the Clyde between Glasgow and Rutherglen.

Following his return from America, Daniel had rented two houses in the Salt Market in Glasgow, for which the sum of £93 Scots covered the rent for a year and a half,[‡] before making the purchase of Shawfield in 1708.[§] He paid the sum of £4,000 sterling for the estate and was thereafter to be known as Campbell of Shawfield, or often, Shaufield.[¶] This property had long belonged

---

*   GD406/1/7141, 25 January 1706.
†   Calendar of Treasury Papers, vol. CVII, p. 41.
‡   About £7 sterling.
§   In correspondence amongst the Hamilton family usually written as 'Ruglen'.
¶   This can become confusing since the house he was to build in the City of Glasgow in 1711 is always referred to as the 'Shawfield Mansion'.

to a branch of the powerful Hamilton family* but, having fallen on hard times, they sold Shawfield and moved to Ireland.† The house then changed hands several times in a very short period before Daniel bought it from Sir Alexander Anstruther of Newark. Thus, despite the fact that it had long been a Hamilton house, Daniel had not even bought it from a member of the family; it is hard to see quite why the Dukes were so vitriolic. One letter in the Hamilton manuscript is from Lord Selkirk to his brother, the Duke, saying he is doing all he can to keep the Campbells out of Clydesdale but that Daniel had obtained an 'interest' in Rutherglen.‡ There is another letter in which the Dowager Duchess of Hamilton, swears she will oust Daniel from Rutherglen.

As Daniel's fortune grew, he moved on from Shawfield (although he always bore it in his name), giving the estate in 1728 to his oldest son and heir, John. There is no image to be found of the house§ and the location of the property in Rutherglen is now occupied by the Shawfield Stadium home to greyhound racing.

Daniel may not have been an MP between 1708 and 1716, but it must have been during this period that he forged his strong friendship with Robert Walpole. Walpole, then serving as Secretary at War was expelled from the House of Commons in 1711 charged with treason. The charge may have been trumped up: the Tories were 'resolved to put [Walpole] out of the way of disturbing them in the House' and the Accounts Commissioners managed to find a means of doing so. Evidently, when making forage contracts for the army in Scotland in 1709 and 1710, Walpole had awarded a share to his kinsman and man of business, one Robert Mann. Mann had in turn agreed to resign his share to the other contractors, who were all Scotsmen, on payment of 500 guineas compensation. One of the contractors, John Montgomerie, gave evidence that Walpole had never intended Mann's appointment but had used it as a means by which he could extract money from the other contractors. Mann denied this, saying that the initiative had come from the contractors themselves who were said to have paid Mann 500 guineas to stay out. This had been done for two contracts.¶ However, since the main contractor who had negotiated with Walpole and Mann was now dead, and Montgomerie's evidence was dismissed as 'hearsay', this charge could not be proven. The evidence on which Walpole was eventually to be convicted showed that Mann's compensation had been paid by means of a note to Walpole and that the first note had been returned with Walpole's signature on it. Mann

---

* The Dukes of Abercorn of Baron's Court, Co. Tyrone, are direct descendants of these Hamiltons.
† *Old Country Houses of Old Glasgow Gentry*, LXXXVIII, Shawfield.
‡ GD406/1/7141, January 1706.
§ The illustration in *Old Glasgow Houses and their Owners* is patently of a later eighteenth-century building, although probably constructed on the same site.
¶ Plumb, *The Making of a Statesman*, pp. 178-80.

protested that he had received all the money himself* but the Commissioners insisted that the receipt proved Walpole had directly benefited.[†]

Found guilty, Walpole was immediately expelled from the Chamber and committed to the Tower, being told to present himself there the following day. The friend who accompanied him to his imprisonment is said to have been Daniel Campbell. According to Lady Mary Wortley Montague he was 'the one personal friend only who walked with him to the Tower Gates'.[‡] She wrote that Walpole never ceased to show his appreciation to Daniel; Walpole's 'staunch friendship and gratitude that ever afterwards he would more readily concede a favour asked by Campbell than by his most powerful supporters ...'.[§]

Some years later, when Walpole was in power as the first British Prime Minister, a satirical ballad was written of the haughty Duke of Argyll. The scene is placed at one of the arrogant ducal levees. All is proud pomp:

> When lo!
> Great Daniel showed his face
> At sight of him bowed low the peer;
> Daniel vouchsafed a nod,
> 'I've seen Sir Robert and 'tis done'[¶]

Stirling Taylor presents the argument that Walpole would not have made his long friendship for Daniel so obvious if it had reminded him of a disreputable event in his early life. In any event, as far as his imprisonment for treason was concerned, it seems far more likely that on this occasion Walpole was careless over his repayment of the £1,000 owing to Mann rather than truly culpable of treasonable behaviour. He spent six months in the Tower. One cannot excuse some of Walpole's actions during his long tenure of power but he has to be acknowledged as a master where finance was concerned; the accusations of corruption were, however, to stick to him throughout his public life.

Walpole bought a house in Chelsea in 1722. It was in the stable yard of the Royal Hospital and had been built in 1690. The stables were at the western end of the hospital on the site where the National Army Museum now stands.** It was a grand house known as the Orangery. Apparently, so much State business came to be conducted in the house at Chelsea that some called Walpole the 'Chelsea Monarch'. The house remained standing,

---

* Robert Mann was a very loyal servant to Walpole. He aided his patron in many illegal or doubtful ventures including the smuggling of dutiable goods on a significant scale. Apparently during the debate in the House of Commons, nobody pointed out that Robert Mann was Walpole's banker; in fact, he had often lent the latter large sums of money and Walpole later rewarded him with the Deputy Treasurership of the Royal Hospital Chelsea.

† Much of this comes from Walpole's entry in the *DNB*.

‡ Letters of the Lady Mary Wortley Montague.

§ *Ibid.*, p. 118.

¶ Taylor, *Robert Walpole*, p. 118.

** After most of the house was destroyed, the site was used for the Royal Hospital's infirmary and evidently the large reception room on the ground floor became Ward 7—see *Chelsea* by Thea Holme.

at least in part, until 1810. Its location was within a stone's throw of what is now Shawfield Street, a Scottish name, and it does not seem unreasonable to conclude that Great Daniel may have had a house there, too, especially since he held a Power of Attorney for the Royal Hospital. At that time, this area of Chelsea was largely given over to smallholdings growing vegetables and fruit for the City and the air was considered to be pure, leading some prominent citizens to move there to escape the filth of the City.

The election of 1715 was a rough affair. Despite the influence wielded by the great landowners such as Montrose and Argyll, the burgh councillors could not always be relied upon to toe their patron's line and they sometimes acted independently. This can be seen clearly in the elections of 1714-16. There was also a growing number of 'merchant princes', such as Daniel, wishing to have their say. The Duke of Montrose had spent much of his youth in Glasgow where his mother, the Dowager Duchess, had both a house and considerable influence, and the Duke himself had attended Glasgow University. In addition, he had vast estates in the vicinity of the city, of which he also held the Barony as a feudal jurisdiction, giving him control over a good part of it.* He was both well known and powerful. Provost Rodgers, who had been elected in 1708 (to Daniel's disgust) threw his weight behind Montrose's candidate, Thomas Smith,† a wealthy merchant, who had been elected in 1710 and, reportedly, was an effective member. Whether this meant that he supported the party line of his patron, Montrose, or that of the Burgh Councillors is another question. It is most probably that he acted principally with his own interests in mind!

The other candidate also counting on the support of his Clan Chief was, of course, Daniel. However, he was, yet again, to be disappointed. The very real threat of a Jacobite rebellion, together with the recent accession of George I to his rather shaky throne, seems to have led the two great Whig Chiefs, Montrose and Argyll, to bury the hatchet for a short period, leading Argyll to lend rather feeble support to Smith. A quantity of correspondence exists in the Graham Papers, Montrose Muniments, in the National Archives of Scotland on this subject. A letter dated 2 October 1714, from Montrose to William Boyle, brother of the Earl of Glasgow, says he fears he may have offended Argyll by exposing the fraudulent behaviour of Daniel as Collector of Customs at the Port of Glasgow.‡ In the event, Argyll wrote to Daniel requesting his support for Smith but Daniel chose to ignore his chief and to pursue his own course; he was defeated. The Argyll faction were lukewarm in their support for Smith but did not wish to give the Jacobites any fuel for stirring up dissent. Smith retained his seat but died almost immediately in January 1716 and the *entente cordiale* between the two Dukes ended.

---

* Sunter, *Patronage and Politics in Scotland, 1707-1832*, p. 199.
† Could this have been the same Thomas Smith who was a partner with Daniel in the smuggling affair of the tide waiters?
‡ NAS, GD220/5/386.

Changes in the Glasgow council in late 1715, had resulted in 'some of Shawfield's particular friends being thrown out not by accident but by design',* but Argyll's conduct during the '15 greatly endeared him to the people of Glasgow, and they regarded him as the saviour of their city. As soon as the Earl of Mar had raised the Jacobite standard,[†] Argyll was sent north to head an army.[‡] His letters to Lord Townshend in London demonstrate a degree of shrewdness as to the situation, coupled with real anxiety.[§] He may have been an aristocrat but he was also evidently a practical man and a good soldier. He feared that, his force being so heavily outnumbered, the Jacobite army might break through into the north of England.

Daniel's eldest brother, Angus, who had inherited Skipness, also played a useful military role in the '15. After inheriting from his father in 1707, Angus is recorded as being one of the gentleman heritors of Argyll, who assembled at Inveraray on 11 August 1715 to sign an oath of loyalty to King George and to raise the fencible men of the shire in preparation for any possible Jacobite rebellion. This foresight was to prove very useful when, several weeks later, the Earl of Mar raised the rebel standard at Braemar on 6 September.

By mid-October when the militia of the shire were called to arms, Angus was in command of two subalterns, two serjeants and 62 men—a not inconsiderable number.[¶] It is probable that he was part of a force of 1,000 Campbells who held Inveraray against a far larger Jacobite force, including the notorious Rob Roy MacGregor (whose mother was a Campbell), and who tried to penetrate the defences before being seen off by a volley of musket fire. Soon after this incident, the Jacobites moved away in search of easier pickings before their final dispersal following the Battle of Sheriffmuir, where the Duke of Argyll gained the upper hand, despite an inconclusive battle.

In late 1715 in Glasgow, Smith's unexpected death heralded a new round of campaigning, with the Montrose faction now having no obvious candidate. Professor Stirling, Principal of Glasgow University, wrote to Montrose 'ther's a great penury of men tolerably fitt'.** Daniel had no doubt as to his own fitness and this time he did have the support of his Clan Chief, whereas Montrose's choice for candidate lay between former Provost John Aird of Glasgow, previously quite close to Argyll, and the incumbent Provost Bowman. Montrose wrote to his cousin, Gorthie, saying of Aird '... they don't call him DC bar that I know no other difference'.[††] It could, however, be safely said that Aird was no Daniel Campbell. The former although ambitious, was lethargic

*　GD220/5/529, Prof. Charles Morthland of Glasgow University to Montrose's cousin and agent, Mungo Gorthie.
†　Mar earned the nickname of 'bobbing John' for his frequent changes of side. He died in exile in Aix la Chapelle despite some efforts to obtain a pardon for him.
‡　Brown, *History of Scotland*, vol. III, p. 172.
§　Tayler, 'John Duke of Argyll', *SHR*, vol. xxvi.
¶　Campbell of Airds, *Clan Campbell*, vol. 3, pp. 106, 108.
**　GD220/5/620.
††　GD220/5/818.

and not very clever. Bowman thought that Rutherglen, the returning Burgh, would stand behind him 'except Shawfield bribe highly'.* It soon became apparent that this was what had happened; Daniel's pockets were deep. Montrose grumbled to Gorthie, who had run a rather lucklustre campaign, that their efforts had been ruined by the vain and ambitious Provost Aird's determination to be elected. Daniel had run his campaign energetically, carefully and by the judicious bestowal of *douceurs*. Such was the bitterness of the Montrose feeling against Daniel, that Gorthie wrote, 'rather than DC have it, I rather ten times Aird had it'. A vain hope. Daniel duly took his seat for the Glasgow Burghs at Westminster and was to hold it, albeit with some considerable difficulty in 1726, until 1734.

In the Parliament that followed his election in 1716, there are few references to his activities, but the Burgh Records of Glasgow have an entry concerning Daniel's representations to Parliament for the renewing and continuing the Act 'for the touns two pennies on the pynt of ale for a further space of years'. The Act was created in recognition of the services the City of Glasgow had rendered to the Crown by its 'loyalty and zeal for the reformed religion ... and more particularly by furnishing at the charge of the inhabitants, considerable numbers of men, well armed and disciplined not only for the defence of that city but even for the support and defence of the government in other places ...'.† In connection with this, Daniel had requested the Magistrates send him two hogsheads of 'Obryan' wine for the 'use of some friends of the touns'. A shipment was arranged and was taken to London by Daniel's brother, Captain Matthew. The costs which added up to a total of £73 12s 5d sterling included freight, corks, casks, customs house officers and bottling charges which seems expensive.‡ It was another case of Daniel knowing which palms to grease.

The following year a record confirms that Daniel Campbell had succeeded in obtaining the renewal of the act of '2d on the pynt in favours of the toun for sixteen years longer after the present gift expyres ...'.§ Perhaps the Burgh officers felt that their expenditure had been worthwhile.

On 7 November 1719 the Burgh Records Proceedings relate that their power of attorney granted to Daniel Campbell in October 1718, had proved successful and that he had succeeded in 'uplifting and getting up for the toun the £736 13s 5d sterling money dew by the government to the toun for the maintenance of the rebell prisoners ...'.¶ Since the magistrates went on to grant Daniel the sum of £348 1s 3d in full payment for his 'pain and trouble', it would seem that he had, once again, also done quite well for himself.

In the elections of May 1722, Daniel was returned again for the Glasgow Burghs, the returning Burgh being the City of Glasgow, itself. On this

* GD220/5/628.
† Glasgow Burgh Records, vol. iv, 1716, p. 677.
‡ Extracts from the Glasgow Burgh Records, vol. iv, 1716, p. 601.
§ *Ibid.*, p. 623.
¶ *Ibid.*, 1719, p. 70.

occasion, he was apparently unopposed. Events were to be very different at the next election in 1726. This followed shortly after the infamous Glasgow Riots, when the name of Daniel Campbell was one of opprobrium to many—see Chapter 7. An opposing candidate, John Blackwood, was put up against him. Wodrow, the famous contemporary society writer and essayist, wrote of Blackwood:

> It's said that Mr. Blackwood has a great party for him in the House; the whole Navy, the Army, the Speaker, and his naming the King in his speech, seems to speak his allouance. But Shawfeild's friends are extremely busy, and represent him as the Scotsman to who England is most indebted; that he had a great share in the Union; that he discofered the frauds of the trade of Glasgou, so much to the prejudice of England; that he brought on the malt-tax in Scotland which releived them of so much money as near comes to one hundred thousand pounds a year etc. Hou farr these wil go, nobody can tell.[*]

The election eventually resulted in a 'double return' but, according to the Glasgow Records, 'the indenture by which John Blackwood was returned was taken off the file by order of the House dated March 1728'[†] and Daniel was awarded the seat on a technicality. Daniel carrying the day seems to have finally been secured as the result of a long speech made by Sir Robert Walpole (Sir RW in Wodrow's correspondence) which was said to be the first time the Prime Minister had done such a thing during an election. Wodrow, who was always ready with a good story to vilify Daniel, wrote that when the news arrived in Glasgow, 'Shawfield's friends' went to Govan where they drank very hard and wrote a letter of congratulation to him. They also evidently got a Mr William Wisheart very drunk and he signed the letter of congratulation when he should have been attending a meeting of the Synod. The party, according to Wodrow, got so inebriated that they were 'caryed into a boat and taken to Glasgou'.[‡]

Daniel stood again in 1734 but by now the Duke of Argyll had withdrawn his support, having probably been offended by Daniel's increasing self-sufficiency, which caused Wodrow to write that he considered that he could 'stand on his oun legges'. During the campaign, some of Daniel's friends rather rashly 'raised a mutiny in the town [Edinburgh] by setting up for themselves and boasting that they had the superior favour with Sir Robert Walpole'.[§] Daniel may have been a close personal friend of Walpole, but it did him no favours on this occasion. A letter to Mungo Graham of Gorthie from William Colquhoun of Garscadder, Glasgow reads, 'the Town of Glasgow will be well pleased Blytheswood [Colin Campbell] will agree to stand and that he and the Provost of Dumbarton assure the town Shawfield will not be

---

[*] Wodrow, *Analecta*, pp. 477, 478.
[†] *Ibid.*, p. 588.
[‡] *Ibid.*, p. 494, 495.
[§] Newcastle (Clumber) MS, letter from Argyll to Pelham.

the member'.* In the event, it was neither Daniel nor Colin but yet another Campbell, William, who was to be elected. William Campbell (1710-87) was a soldier and cousin to the Duke of Argyll, though as Glasgow's Member of Parliament, he was evidently a failure. A letter from one of his constituents explains why William was not selected to serve any longer: '... he wrote only three letters to this Corporation [Glasgow] in seven years and he did not so much as know who were our Magistrates for† his first letter was addressed to Richard Graham as Provost of the Town ...'.

There is no further record of Daniel seeking election but his descendants certainly did so. The Duke of Montrose wrote to Gorthie in 1745:

> the tyme will come when the family [the Grahams] will have sones, will it not then be judged a little money now laid out will be of singular service, tho' Shawfield and Argyll are not all one now they will soon agree, forbidd it heaven, I ever see the Campbells command Stirlingshyre.‡

His forecast was more accurate than he could have known. With John Campbell of Shawfield and Islay later marrying the 5th Duke's daughter, Lady Charlotte, there was presumably a rapprochement between these two branches of the Clan.

Daniel's brother, John, served as member for Edinburgh from 1721-34, his career as an MP ending as a result of determined and successful efforts to evict both brothers from the House, which was promoted by Montrose and his allies. In several reference books, such as the *Dictionary of National Biography* and *House of Commons*,§ John is listed as being unmarried, but a genealogist of this branch of Campbell Clan¶ has found that he did indeed marry Elizabeth Leckie in 1701, probably a sister of Great Daniel's first wife, Margaret Leckie. John and his wife had three daughters and a son, Colin.** John was also involved in trading, frequently in conjunction with brothers Daniel and Matthew. As Lord Provost of Edinburgh in 1715, he is credited with having saved the city from the rebels in the Jacobite rebellion, by his prompt summoning of military help in the form of the Duke of Argyll, who marched from Stirling to protect the city. The position of Lord Provost was, in itself, very significant since it bestowed control of the city and any military forces within it, on the incumbent. John Campbell was an active and successful man.††

* GD220/5/1302.
† *History of the House of Commons*; Caldwell papers ii(1) p. 62.
‡ GD220/5/1609.
§ Romney and Sedgewick, *House of Commons 1715-1754*, OUP, 1970.
¶ Catriona Bourdillon, née Campbell.
** I think it is this Colin to whom his uncle, Daniel, was to leave the property of Ardentinny.
†† There are references to John having also been Groom of the Bedchamber and Master of Works. I think that the first post confuses him with another John Campbell who was married to a lady 'housekeeper' in one of the royal palaces, Somerset House, and the second with John Campbell of Mamore, Chamberlain to the Duke of Argyll. Trying to keep the Campbell Johns, Walters and Colins in their correct pigeon holes is no easy task!

5

The Equivalent & Aspects of
Early Banking in Scotland

Scotland has been compared to Holland with regard to early banking: two Calvinistic countries struggling with obstacles of nature. By the end of the seventeenth century, merchants in England and Scotland were aware of the Dutch capacity to use paper transactions in trading exchanges in the same manner as they used coin. However, people in general, and in Scotland in particular, were to remain highly suspicious of paper for many years. This led to a constant shortage of coin and ready cash.

Prior to 1640, banking was done entirely via goldsmiths and the more prosperous merchants. Borrowers and lenders entered into private contracts which were usually drawn up by a lawyer and entered officially in the books of local notaries. Dependence on the goldsmiths for ready cash, together with a secure place to deposit both coin and precious items, arose from 1640 when Charles I, desperate for money, seized the reserves of many merchants which had been deposited in the Tower of London. This was in an effort to blackmail them into making him a loan. Needless to say, the merchants were outraged and, from that date on, until the foundation of what we would consider to be true banking institutions, they chose to entrust all their holdings of gold and silver to the goldsmiths.

The most frequent security was, of course, land; there was no other real alternative in Scotland at the time. This form of security gave Daniel Campbell the opportunity to acquire three of his properties: Woodhall, Shawfield and, ultimately, Islay. He was never a man to pass up a good opportunity and lent to many of the great in his day including his first patrons, the 1st and 2nd Dukes of Argyll.* What security the Dukes offered is not recorded in the Shawfield manuscript; possibly it was just their backing for Daniel's efforts to obtain a seat in Parliament, a post in the Customs, and a position as Commissioner for the Act of Union.

By the last decade of the seventeenth century, the expansion of world trade and the need to finance the almost continuous wars with France had led to the growth of the London money market, but the Government found itself unable to service its debt to the goldsmiths. Many schemes were mooted

---

* He had already paid for the funeral of the 1st Duke.

but all failed until that enterprising Scot, William Paterson, proposed a 'Bank of England'* and a 'fund for perpetual interest' which eventually became law. Paterson was joined in this enterprise by Charles Montagu, Chancellor of the Exchequer, and Michael Godfrey, a powerful City merchant. The public was able to invest in the Bank and their subscriptions formed the capital for the original Bank of England.

The principal problem for Scotland was how to establish long term credit at a reasonable rate and how to increase the amount of 'specie', or coin, in circulation. In cash-starved 'North Britain' there could be no such scheme as that devised by Paterson, but some resourceful gentlemen did come up with the idea of the Bank of Scotland, as a publicly owned bank. The Bank of Scotland received its statutory credentials on 17 July 1695 and opened its doors for business the following year with the very small capital of £100,000. A Scottish Act of Parliament stipulated that no other bank could be opened for a further 21 years, although the Darien Company began to trade in much the manner of a bank, albeit with no more success than its ill-fated expedition. The Bank of Scotland was initially created to aid and promote Scottish business but, unfortunately, a few years later, its management chose to give assistance in raising money for the Jacobites in the '15 and this led to the bank losing its monopoly the following year, in 1716.

Following the failure of both the Darien Expedition, together with its 'bank', and at the moment when Union was appearing to be the sole, if unpalatable, solution, an Act of the Scottish Parliament, with Daniel Campbell as a representative for the burghs, voted that £234,884 5s ¾d to be paid out to compensate the unfortunate Darien subscribers. This payment was not made immediately and was then overtaken by the creation of the Equivalent in 1707.

Where would this sum have come from? With serious negotiations for Union underway, the question never arose. The 15th Article of the Treaty of Union stipulated that England would pay Scotland the 'Equivalent' as it was somewhat misleadingly designated. This was calculated at a sum of £398,085 10s. to compensate the Darien shareholders, to cover the rather lavish expenses of the Commissioners who had debated and drafted the Treaty of Union, to pay overdue salaries to the army and other officials, to reimburse people who might have lost out during the re-coinage that was necessary,[†] and to alleviate the problems which were anticipated in Scotland when taxation levels were eventually brought into line with the higher English level. There was also to be the even more extraordinary Arising Equivalent which was to be made up from the anticipated increase in tax revenue. How would the Equivalent be estimated? In the records of the Equivalent Company held in the archives of The Royal Bank of Scotland, there are detailed comparisons between the duty paid

---

* www.bankofengland.co.uk/about/history/timeline.htm
† A wide variety of coinage was in use in Scotland at the time.

in Scotland on specified items: wine, whale fins, plantation duty, sale of lottery tickets, tobacco, duty on clerks, apprentices, candles, etc., with that raised by England. When tallied, this demonstrated that Scotland only contributed around three percent of the amount levied by England.

England   £104,623 14s 0d
Scotland   £3,699

Several weeks after the Act of Union came into being on 1 May 1707, the Equivalent money had still not arrived in Edinburgh. The Scots were furious. Finally, in August, an imposing convoy of 12 wagons, each drawn by six horses, lumbered into the city. The ponderous cavalcade had taken six weeks to travel from London. It rapidly transpired that only £100,000 was in 'specie', the remainder being in Bank of England notes and Exchange bills payable in London. Notes and exchange bills drawn on London were not much use to the people of Scotland who, in any event, mistrusted pieces of paper, and the Commissioners for the Equivalent were forced to send to London for more 'coyne'.

The variety of coinage in use in Scotland at the time was extraordinary. It included a wide diversity of foreign silver valued at much more than the existing Scottish coins. Some of the English coins dated from the Plantaganet era.[*] All had to be assessed by the Burgh magistrates who would then give the owner a certificate as 'to what loss he would sustain by their transformation into coins of English standard'.[†] This was then taken to the Equivalent Commissioners for reimbursement. Daniel was one of the first Commissioners for the Equivalent. It has been impossible to discover when he ceased in this role but it may have been following the investigation of his dealings at the Scottish Customs.

The Archives of The Royal Bank contain an account of payments made by the Commissioners of the Equivalent to themselves, the Commissioners for the Union, Secretaries and 'accompants' for the two treaties of Union.[‡] There are 32 names listed, some of these men had worked through both negotiations. For the first short and unsuccessful negotiations in 1702, Scottish peers received £500 and for the considerably more protracted but ultimately successful negotiations in 1706, £1,000. Commoners received £500 for the successful Treaty[§] but there were some peculiar figures; for example, Alexander Grant the Younger was awarded the odd sum of £498 12s 2d.

In 1709, Daniel received a payment of £178 15s[¶] from the Equivalent Office which was probably interest due on a debenture, at a rate of 5 per cent

---

[*] *History of The Royal Bank of Scotland*, p. 25.
[†] *Ibid.*
[‡] RBS EQ22/20.
[§] Daniel's payment appears as No. 27 in CEQ 30/2.
[¶] RBS EQ 23/24.

p.a. for payment from 24 June 1708. He assigned this to John Buchanan, Jr by an endorsement on the reverse side. The archives of The Royal Bank of Scotland contain a number of other similar payments to people, many slips having been endorsed several times. Most of these payments were approved by the Lords Commissioner of the Treasury: the Earls of Glasgow, Northesk and Forfar and commoner, Hugh Montgomerie. It seems likely that Daniel accepted Government debentures in the place of a cash repayment on his Darien investment. There are further notes of odd sums being paid into his Equivalent account, one of £61 9s 4d and another of £92 16s 5d. By the time he transferred his Equivalent stock into the newly formed Royal Bank of Scotland in 1727, the sum amounted to £6,010 15s 3d.* It has been necessary to be very cautious when attributing payments to a 'Daniel Campbell' between the Equivalent and The Royal Bank. 'Great' Daniel was certainly involved in several transactions but most of those arising in the name of a Daniel Campbell, were those of the Secretary of the Royal Bank, who, while holding the same name and obviously of the same Clan, was not a close relation as far as one can determine.

There is little information to be found concerning Daniel's other banking activities in Scotland which is probably more due to the absence of records than to a lack of activity. A company called Campbell and Crawford had a trading account with the Bank of Scotland; this was almost certainly the company of Daniel Campbell and Matthew Crawford. Crawford was one of Daniel's most significant partners over many years. Unfortunately, the Bank's records for that date are incomplete and there is no record of their transactions in the archives.

There are fortunately some snippets of information relating to Daniel's English banking activities which mainly come from the archives of Messrs Coutts and Co. and Drummonds Bank.† The former was founded by John Campbell, originally apprenticed to a goldsmith, John Threeplaid (or Thripland) in Edinburgh. This John Campbell was indeed a first cousin to Daniel. He was the son of either Colin (hanged in 1685) or his brother, Angus,‡ and, as such, well known to Daniel and his brothers. He had arrived in London by 1692§ and established himself at the Three Crowns in the Strand.¶ Here he was well situated for the Court and thus for his noble clients, most of whom were prominent Whigs. The first ledgers that survive in Coutts' archives date from 1712 but from the Bank's Letterbooks, dating from 1699, there exists an exchange of letters between John Campbell and George Middleton (following John's death in 1712) and Daniel. These letters, which continue until 1720, appear to be only a small part of a considerable correspondence. In addition to

---

*   RBS EEQ/14.
†   Coutts and Co. is one of the world's oldest commercial banks. Both banks are now part of The Royal Bank of Scotland.
‡   Brother Angus had succeeded to the lairdship of Skipness in 1702.
§   Healey, *Coutts and Co., Portrait of a Private Bank*, p. 7.
¶   The 'Three Crowns' is still used by Coutts on cheque books and other items.

lending money, John Campbell seems to have acted as a sort of London agent for some of his customers. In 1708, he frequently refers to Daniel's brother, Matthew. This was at one of the periods when Matthew had been captured by the French: '... very sorry for the bad news I hear of Captain Matthew's being taken by the French wch I heard yesterday at the Admiralty. I long to hear the particulars ... doubt not but he hath acquitted honourably ...'.[*] In a second letter he writes 'I am sorry to hear yr brother is not relieved ... but it seems there is severalls ... in the same s[itua]ation'. Matthew evidently had to wait more than two months in captivity, once in Dinard and once in St Malo, because there were several Captains who had been seized before him and who also had to be 'relieved', presumably meaning ransomed or exchanged.

On 1 January 1708/9,[†] John referred to a ship belonging to Daniel that has brought in wine and brandy some of which has been entrusted to John's care: 'I have often been trusted wt money but never wt good liquor before ... how honest I shall bee I know not however I shall always drink yr health.' A letter written two weeks later says that he has been sampling the wine with Daniel's landlord: 'The wine is tolerable and I did drink 5 bottles amongst 4 and the next day I was oblidged to keep my head ...'!

In 1710, John wrote that he wanted to know the degree of success Daniel had experienced in those ships that sailed to Guinea from Glasgow since Union, requesting Daniel send him a letter with this information to show 'the members what success you have had'. Does this refer to members of a syndicate investing in such ships? We know that as owner of one of the four sugar houses in Glasgow, Daniel shipped spirits to Guinea.

By 1708, in addition to having been a working goldsmith and now a banker, John was also army paymaster and responsible for the accounts of the army in Dumbarton, Stirling and Edinburgh. We read of his dealings with several Scottish regiments such as the Duke of Argyll's Regiment of Horse. The Duke and his brother, Ilay, were, of course, Bank customers but ones that could be a headache since they were perpetually short of cash. In a letter dated November 1708, addressed to Daniel, John bemoans the shortage of 'coine' in London saying that he has a good deal of money to bring from Edinburgh but 'can find no occasion at present'—presumably he could not find anyone honest enough to bring it.

This letter also refers to annuities which were becoming very popular. Parliament enacted hundreds of laws to pay for its wars and from 1709 lotteries were introduced to fund public works, wars and so forth. Until the end of the eighteenth century, prizes were paid out in the form of terminable or perpetual annuities. Loans could also be raised against lottery tickets. This form of annuity became especially popular amongst the upper classes and John refers to them in several of his letters. In one, dated 23 May 1710, he

---

* Coutts Archives, letter dated 15 May 1708.
† Both OS and NS dates are given in the document.

refers to the loss of one of Daniel's ships[*] and hopes that he will have better success in the lottery to be drawn in August. He goes on to explain how the lottery is drawn:

> ... I am informed the method of drawing is the blanks are all put into one box mixed with ye benefits and ye tickits in another box and tow boys draws one takes out a ticket and another blank or benift which comes to his hand and then its entered by the severll clarkes and printed[†]

In 1711 John wrote that he had sold Daniel's 'Lotterie tickits' and his 'affrecan' stock since 'I was loath to delay longer least the price of both should sink'.[‡]

In December 1712, George Middleton, now a partner in the Bank and husband of John's daughter Mary, wrote to Daniel telling him of his father-in-law's death and saying that he had taken over the business. At the time of his death, John Campbell had some twenty to thirty Scottish peers as customers, most of whom were Whigs and supporters of the Hanoverian succession. Following this date, there are only a few surviving letters concerning Great Daniel. With the development of a more modern banking business, the Goldsmiths' original business declined.

Perhaps Daniel switched his account to Drummonds. He is mentioned in that bank's archives as having an account between 1723 and 1739. Drummonds was founded by another Scot, Andrew Drummond in 1717.[§] His address in London is given as 'at the Golden Eagle, Charing Cross'. In common with John Campbell, Drummond had been apprenticed in Edinburgh before riding to London, 'with only 10 guineas in his pocket'. He worked very hard as a silversmith but, 'on Sunday I put on a good coat and sword and kept company that drank claret'.[¶] The Drummond ledgers also record the names of several ships in which Daniel had an interest (though he was not necessarily the sole owner), indicating that he was still trading overseas until at least 1733. There are also many transactions dealing with 'plate'. In April 1721, for example, Daniel spent £119 10s 8d on plate which included 'wrought' plate (presumably objects made in silver), or sometimes gilt, 'unwrought' plate and also 'dymonds'.[**] There are also several records of payments to redeem bonds and receipt of payments of prize money.

In 1723 the Equivalent Society was incorporated as the Equivalent Company. The South Sea Bubble[††] had collapsed leaving thousands of people

---

* This was probably the *Concord*, seized from Capt. Dugald Campbell by a privateer in the Mediterranean.
† Coutts and Co. Archives, letter from JC to DC dated 23 May 1710.
‡ *Ibid.*
§ His elder brother, William, was a Jacobite who fought in the '15 and the '45, when he died in battle.
¶ Drummonds ledgers, vol. II, p. 299.
** DR 426/1; DR 427/15, /16, /17, /18.
†† The South Sea debt to December 1713 was considered to be debt contracted prior to Union.

bankrupt. Robert Walpole became Prime Minister and, backed by prominent Whigs including Argyll, Ilay, Daniel, George Drummond and Daniel's brother, John, Lord Provost of Edinburgh, Walpole wielded great power and influence in Scotland. There is even a record of the King investing the sum of £3,000 in the Equivalent Company in 1725. The Charter granted to The Royal Bank of Scotland on 31 May 1727, was of great assistance to Walpole in his attempts to gain political control of Scotland. The Equivalent Company and The Royal Bank ran more or less in tandem in 1727. With the flotation of The Royal Bank that year, the new directors had to transfer their Equivalent stock into the new bank.

In theory, the Equivalent Company and The Royal Bank of Scotland remained separate institutions but relations between the two were always close and many principal employees of one also worked for the other. It was not until 1851 that the Equivalent Company was finally dissolved. Many people over the years must have wondered at the name of this peculiar institution. When the day for dissolution finally arrived, the Edinburgh records were transferred to The Royal Bank and the board announced that 'to no establishment could the trust be with more propriety confided than to that of its eminent offspring, The Royal Bank of Scotland'.[*]

---

[*] *The Archive Guide of the RBS–The Equivalent Company.*

6

Great Daniel's Family and Properties

Great Daniel had married Margaret Leckie on his return from the Americas in 1694, and she bore him six surviving children: John, Walter, Daniel, Margaret, Jannet and Anne. Margaret died in 1711 and Daniel remarried in 1714. In the same way that the status of his first marriage had matched his new found prosperity and ensured his entry into the Glasgow mercantile elite, Daniel's second marriage reflected his rising social status. His second wife was Lady Katherine Erskine Denholm, widow of Sir William Denholm Bt of Westshields and daughter of Henry Erskine, Lord Cardross, heir to the Earl of Buchan. This was one of Scotland's grandest families and Daniel recognised the importance of joining his name to that of such a dynasty. The marriage was of mutual benefit, as his new in-laws were only too anxious to get their hands on some of Daniel's fortune in order to ameliorate their own diminished circumstances. Sir William had evidently died deeply in debt, and Daniel found himself required to 'bail out' his new wife as one of Sir William's heirs. Furthermore, Daniel's new brother-in-law, David, Earl of Buchan, in writing to felicitate him on his marriage to his sister, touched him for £250 in the same letter.

Daniel was evidently frequently called upon to bail out his 'in-laws'; he had already helped several members of the Leckie family. In 1734, Michael and William Leckie both owed Daniel considerable sums of money and in payment William was forced to hand over the Temple lands of Greenside to Daniel's son, Walter who, at the time, was Receiver General of HM Customs in Scotland.

Daniel's eldest son, John, married Lady Margaret Campbell, daughter of the Earl of Loudon; they had no children and she died young in 1733. He then married the Lady Henrietta (Hennriet) Cunninghame, daughter of the Earl of Glencairn* and they had three sons: John, Daniel and Walter. John did not have an uneventful life; thanks to his father's influence, he served as a Commissioner for the Revenue. In the Montrose papers there is a letter, dated 7 July 1721, from Mungo Graham of Gorthie to Charles Morthland of Glasgow University, saying that Shawfield has obtained a post for John in the Customs despite opposition.† This underlines Daniel's growing power

---

* Which is where the frequent use of Glencairn as a name in the family came from.
† GD220/5/989.

and influence; after all it had only been very recently that his own affairs in the Customs for the Port of Glasgow had been exposed as not exactly whiter than white!

Great Daniel and Katherine had a daughter, Katherine, and two other children who do not appear to have survived infancy. Their daughter married Thomas Gordon of Earlston and Airds in 1737. The couple soon found themselves in severe financial difficulties. Great Daniel had given his daughter a dowry of £3,000 on her marriage and the father of the bridegroom, Sir Thomas, had made over his estates to his son. These yielded a rental income of £411 sterling a year of 'free rent' and 'with the burden of debt contained in a List amounting to £4,900 sterling' which, at the time, was understood to be the whole sum of debt due by Sir Thomas.[*] This was, however, rapidly discovered to be far from the truth—the real extent being at least twice this figure. Young Thomas called a meeting of his creditors being quite unable to meet his obligations. Great Daniel was 'prevailed upon to accept of a Disposition of the Estate' which obliged him to pay all the 'real debts' and half the 'personal debts'. This proposition was to be considered extremely fair by all except one of the creditors. The first creditors' meeting was held on 2 February 1743, but the case was not resolved for seven years owing to the obduracy of one Mr Alexander Corson. Corson was considered to have behaved extremely dishonestly and 'with peevishness and bad humour'[†] leading Shawfield to pay out more than had originally been agreed. It is not difficult to arrive at the conclusion that Daniel, although an extremely canny and tough businessman, and not above resorting to some dealings that do not bear close scrutiny, was a very generous and supportive character where family was concerned

As we have seen, Daniel spent long periods in London during the Union negotiations where he had doubtless been introduced to sophisticated contemporary taste in architecture, paintings and furnishings. It was not long, therefore, before he decided to make two further significant investments in property as befitted his new status. The fact that he undertook both of these projects at virtually the same time is confirmation that he had rapidly augmented his fortune.

Shortly after acquiring the Shawfield estate in Rutherglen, and following his elevation as an MP, a Commissioner for the Union and also for the Equivalent, Daniel looked for a larger property outside Glasgow. He purchased the estate of Woodhall, Monklands in the county of Lanarkshire, from Laurence Crauford of Jordanhill. Woodhall had previously been the family home of yet another branch of the Hamilton family. Daniel's papers tell us that in 1711 he purchased a 22-year bond for £25,477 17s, and that the property then yielded an income of £2,428.00.[‡]

---

[*] NAS RH15/3/256A.

[†] Ibid.

[‡] Shawfield MS, 524.

Sketch of Woodhall (Courtesy of the North Lanarkshire Museums Section, Airdrie)

Woodhall was to become the principal family seat and would remain so for more than 130 years. It was the most important and richest of Daniel's estates and in its heyday it was considered one of the finest properties in the west of Scotland. Located just eight miles from Glasgow and only 20 from Edinburgh, the house today would have stood only 200 yards north of the M8, less than half a mile south of Calderbank and a couple of miles south of Airdrie. Daniel never did things by halves and, during his visits to England, as an MP at Westminster and in his growing friendship with Robert Walpole, he must have visited some extraordinary houses and gardens. He certainly began to create what was to become an exceptional garden at Woodhall—a tradition to be maintained by his descendants, who were constantly adding 'improvements' to the landscape.[*]

Woodhall was an impressive estate and well placed as a centre for Daniel's many and diverse activities. Situated on the north bank of the river Calder, the house is described as being of the 'age of Louis XIV'.[†] Today, there remains virtually no trace of the house and most of the estate has been subsumed by the expansion of Glasgow and its satellites—not to mention the M8, M74 and two railway lines which cut right through the heart of the former property. Today one can search in vain throughout the area for any vestige of the estate and only a vivid description remains of what Woodhall must have been like in its heyday.[‡]

Entering via the West Lodge at Thankerton, an avenue stretched for at least a mile and a half until it reached the East Lodge. The estate also

---

[*] Especially Daniel the Younger.
[†] Extracts from the 3rd Statistical Account of Scotland, vol. VI, pp. 783, 785; vol. 16, pp. 316, 328.
[‡] Series L127, 2465 Airdrie Public Library, dated 1961.

included the village of 'Holytoun'. The ornamental gardens, woodlands and lakes of Woodhall, together with vistas unspoilt by virtue of 'sunk fences',* were amongst its most famous features. There were succession houses for peaches, vines and other tropical fruits, heated by an ingenious system, whereby heat and smoke rose from great pits, presumably burning the local coal, through tunnels in the walls to emerge at the top of the glasshouses. The flower gardens were also enclosed by a high wall to shelter them from the elements. Entering via the West Lodge, the first building one encountered was known as 'the Cathedral'. The tower of this building was nothing to do with a church, but merely a vantage point from which spectators could watch horse-racing below.

The estate was also to become famous for the coal and minerals it contained. Perhaps this was the undoing of the house itself, as all the tunnelling led to a problem with subsidence and was probably one of the principal reasons that the building was finally abandoned.[†] The house was originally approached from the north where there were wide, shallow stone steps rising to the main entrance. On these steps, estate pipers would play while the family had their meals.

It was without doubt a grand house, with the large central block flanked by two apparently attached but smaller buildings of no especial merit.[‡] There were, however, two further 'pavilions' detached from the main house. These two 'wings' owe much to the classical Palladian influence which was so much admired by Daniel and Colen Campbell, his architect and distant cousin. It is something of a puzzle as to when these were added as they do not appear on the estate map of 1753. But perhaps the most interesting fact concerning the architecture is that Daniel had a new entrance façade created on the southern side of the house. This frontage was literally placed against what had originally been the rear of the building. It has been described as a most ambitious scheme, if indeed that is what actually had been proposed.[§] This work was probably carried out at much the same time as Daniel was building the Shawfield Mansion in the Trongate in Glasgow (see page 59). The idea has been mooted that the same architect, Colen Campbell, may have been responsible. There are certainly plates showing façades bearing similar features in Colen Campbell's seminal work *Vitruvius Britannicus*.[¶] Another suggestion is that Daniel designed the new front himself following Colen's principles.

The sole criticism concerning the new front seems to have been that some people considered the principal door to be too small for such a grand house.

---

* Presumably a ha-ha.

† It did suffer two fires after sequestration and its sale, but could probably have been rebuilt but for the subsidence.

‡ This is to judge by the old photos still available.

§ See 'The Enigma of Woodhall House' by Kitty Cruft in *Design and Practice in British Architecture*, vol. 27, 1984.

¶ Daniel is listed as having been a subscriber to the first two volumes.

Woodhall as a ruin c.1900 (Photo from the Royal Commission on the Ancient & Historical Monuments of Scotland)

However, the windows were large and the first-floor reception rooms had high ceilings and ornamental alcoves for busts and other decorative objects. The substantial reception room above the entrance was used for entertainment and had a stage. Evidently, theatrical groups were invited to come and entertain guests. The family may also have taken part in these productions and Daniel the Younger, a great dandy in his time, left a large collection of what were described as 'theatrical costumes' in the sale catalogue at the time of the dispersal sales in the mid-nineteenth century. Surmounting the central window on the first floor of the building, was a stone triangle containing a representation of the legendary griffin of Islay holding a sun disc in his forepaws.* This must have been added some years after Daniel had bought the house, after he acquired the island of Islay. The windows of the side wings, were topped by sculptures of a man's head surmounted by three roses.

---

* This is the family crest and was presumably added after Daniel's acquisition of Islay in 1726. See rear endpaper.

'Great' Daniel Campbell of Shawfield and Islay
(Painting property of Michael Hepburne Scott, photograph by Patrick Rafferty)

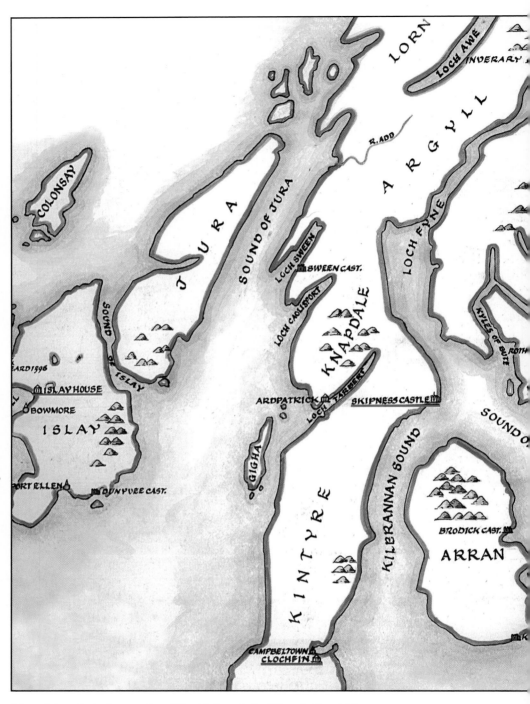

*Map of the principal properties of Daniel Campbell of Shawfield and Islay
(Drawn by Adam Johnstone)*

ARDKINGLAS
PERTH
R. TEITH
R. FORTH
STIRLING
LOCH GOIL
LOCH LOMOND
STIRLING
INNY
LOCH LONG
GARELOCH
DUMBARTON
KYLSYTH
OON
DUMBARTON
RENFREW
PAISLEY
GLASGOW
SHAWFIELD MANSION (N. TRONGATE)
SHAWFIELD ESTATE
RUTHERGLEN
WOODHALL
(HOLYTOWN)
R. CLYDE
FIRTH OF CLYDE
LARGS
CUMBRAE
HAMILTON
LANARK
AYR
LANARK
KILMARNOCK
R. AYR
AST.
AYR
A. T. Johnston 2007

CAMPBELL
of Ardentinny

CAMPBELL
of Skipness

Coats of Arms of the Campbells of Ardentinny,
Campbells of Skipness, Campbells of Shawfield and
Islay, Robert Campbell of Stockholm, Campbells of
Ardpatrick, by Adam Johnstone

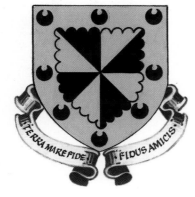

CAMPBELLS
of Shawfield and Islay

ROBERT CAMPBELL
Merchant in Stockholm

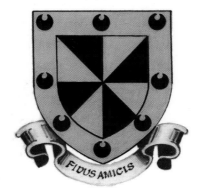

CAMPBELL
of Ardpatrick

Colin Campbell, Captain of Skipness
(Painting property of Francis Hepburne Scott, photograph by Patrick Rafferty)

*Daniel Campbell the Younger
of Shawfield and Islay
(b. c.1737-1777)
(Private collection)*

*John Campbell (d. 1773),
brother of Daniel the
Younger (Private collection)*

John Francis Campbell as a young man (Private collection)

A footnote to this account of Woodhall is that it produced one of history's best known horticulturists, William Aiton. Aiton, the first curator of the great botanical gardens of Kew, was born in the parish and learned his craft while working at Woodhall during Great Daniel's life. It was only a year after Daniel's death, that Aiton went to London in 1754 and was quickly brought to the notice of the Dowager Princess of Wales[*] as a person well qualified to create a great botanical garden at Kew. He worked at Kew for 34 years, dying in 1793. His greatest legacy, after the gardens themselves, was his *Hortus Kewensis*, a work in three volumes.

Daniel had acquired Woodhall, his 'country seat', and had unquestionably expended a vast amount of money on its embellishment, but at the same time, he was also building a house in the city of Glasgow itself: his 'town house'.

The Shawfield Mansion

Highly significant architecturally, the Shawfield Mansion, as it was to become known, is credited with being proof of both the increasing prosperity of Glasgow and the growing wealth of the city's most successful merchants.[†] Daniel chose a site at what was the extreme western edge of the city at that time and bought up numerous small gardens, crofts and yards, consolidating them into a sizeable block. The house faced down a wide street to Glasgow Bridge, with the large rear garden running down to 'Back Cow Loan'—evidently this was a rustic area at the time—at the extreme city limit. In future years, this lane was renamed Ingram Street.[‡]

The early work of the architect, Colen Campbell, shows influence of James Smith, but eventually he was to become rather more famous for dedicating himself to the furtherance of the emerging classical style. Inigo Jones may have introduced the style of Palladio on his return from Italy a hundred years earlier, but it was not to be until the early eighteenth century that this mode became truly appreciated in England and also in Scotland. Campbell embraced the simpler, rational design that turned its back on the elaborate, more massive, Carolingean architecture. In an article 'Colen Campbell's Shawfield Mansion in Glasgow' the author asserts that the house was built in pure William and Mary or Queen Anne style and that it was erected before Campbell came 'under the influence of Palladio'.[§] This is a statement surely open to argument as any inspection of the drawings and engravings can attest. Other authorities call the mansion the first 'Palladian' mansion in Scotland and it was doubly influential due to its inclusion in Colen Campbell's *Vitruvius Britannicus*, which in turn influenced architects not only in Britain but also in the colonies. Colen Campbell's own words

---

[*] Ext. statistical account of Scotland, vol. VI, p. 787 and vol. XVI, p. 316.

[†] Eyre Todd, *History of Glasgow*, vol. iii.

[‡] Mitchell, *Old Glasgow Essays*, p. 18. It was much later also known in the architectural world as the site of the famous tea room designed by Charles Rennie Mackintosh.

[§] Goodfellow, *Colen Campbell's Shawfield Mansion in Glasgow*, pp. 123-7.

describe the house, as he designed it, better than any other commentary:

> Daniel Campbell of Shawfield Esq., has built this house, after my Design,
> in Glasgow, the best situated and regular city in Scotland; the principal
> Apartment is in the first story; the Staircase is so placed in the Middle
> as to serve 4 good Apartments in the second Story; the Front is dressed
> with Rusticks of a large Proportion, and a Dorick cornice and Balustrade,
> the Garrets receive light from the Roof inwardly; the whole Building is of
> good Stone and well-finished. Anno 1712.[*]

There was a wide, gravelled courtyard giving on to the front door and the
house was sited to close the view up Stockwell Street from Glasgow Bridge.
The placing of a house across the end of a broad street was a peculiarly
Glaswegian idea of that era; the eye was led down the street to the glory of
the mansion at the far end, in the same way as an 'eye catcher' would be sited
in a romantic park. The gardens that stretched down to Back Cow Loan,
were extensive, with orchards and flower gardens; the whole was enclosed
by a wall. It was, by far, the grandest house that had been built in Glasgow
(and remained the premier house in the city for at least 50 years). It was
Colen Campbell's first commission and the only house he built in Scotland.
It is a great misfortune that it does not still stand to bear witness to both his
creativity and his patron's taste.

Nowadays Colen Campbell is frequently regarded less highly than some
of his contemporaries, but he was undoubtedly influential and probably at
his best when dealing with houses true to Palladian principles. The Shawfield
Mansion was his first project. Colen was later to be one of several well-known
architects, the best men of their day, to work at Houghton in Norfolk, home
of Robert Walpole. Perhaps Daniel's friendship with the Prime Minister led
to this commission.

The Glasgow mansion featured again, albeit briefly, in 1715 at the time of
the Rebellion. The often rather ineffectual Provost Aird, raised a regiment of
500 men to march and join the Duke of Argyll, who was in command of the
Government Army. The citizens of Glasgow prepared to defend themselves
by digging deep and broad ditches to fortify the town against the rebels. The
Duke subsequently paid a visit to Glasgow and approved the preparations
that had been made. On this visit he stayed at the Shawfield Mansion, both
because it belonged to a fellow Campbell and because it was certainly the
grandest house in town.

York Buildings Company and the Kilsyth Estate

Despite owning a grand town house and country residence, Daniel still had an
eye for the main chance and he was to acquire a further great estate following

---

[*] Colen Campbell's *Vitruvius Britannicus*, vol. 2, plate 51.

the misfortunes of the Livingstons, a family of resolute Jacobites. After the 1715 rebellion, an early property speculator, York Buildings Company, was granted permission by the Government to purchase the forfeited estates of the rebels. York Buildings Company was to become the largest landowner in Scotland, but it never prospered financially owing to poor management; this enraged Daniel, who was an investor, since he knew the lack of success was attributable to inefficiency. York Buildings Company had so many cases heard in litigation that it turned into a sort of 'Jarndyce and Jarndyce' of the eighteenth century and there is probably no lawyer in Scotland who has not come across it in the course of their studies. During the 150 or so years of its existence, the company spent an average of £3,000 per annum on litigation.[*] David Murray wrote 'after an existence of more than 150 years the company came quietly to an end. It had commenced modestly and it expired unnoticed and without regret'.[†] However, some of those who took advantage of the low prices of the estates for sale certainly profited and one of them was Great Daniel.

The Kilsyth estate was the company's second acquisition and was purchased for £16,000. The 3rd Viscount Kilsyth was a well-known Jacobite and had bitterly opposed the Act of Union. He was a member of the longstanding Livingston family in Stirlingshire and had fled abroad following the '15, in debt to the Bank of Scotland and probably to others. The family lost everything. In 1721, the estate was let to one James Stark for 19 years at an annual rental of £800 plus a fifth part of any coal mined. Stark may have been a front man for someone else, such as a member of the Livingston family, but it is impossible to know.[‡] He was further required to plant two trees for each one that he felled and 'to plant oak, elm, ash or fir at the end of every twenty feet in length in all enclosures which he should make'.[§]

Two years later, Stark was bankrupt and he asked York Buildings Company to take the estate off his hands. This they did, appointing him factor. During his service of five years in this capacity, the estate returned a profit of £634 per annum. Some relations of the attainted Viscount Kilsyth then made representations to the company for the purchase of the property. Enter Great Daniel. He represented to the commissioners that to permit the family of the previous owner to buy the estate could prove a danger to the state. He then made a counter offer applying for a 99-year lease for himself. Needless to say, he struck an excellent deal, although it could hardly have been viewed as such by the company. There was an annual rental of £500, which included minerals and he was also relieved of the necessity to plant trees.[¶] The Canny Scot was at work again.

---

[*] Panton, *Kilsyth, a Parish History*.
[†] Murray, *The York Building Company*, p. 111.
[‡] In many cases the son, mother or other close relation of the 'traitor' purchased or rented the house.
[§] Murray, *The York Building Company*, p. 48.
[¶] *Ibid.*

Daniel also opposed Kilsyth's wife, Katherine Walkinshaw, when she appealed to the Lord of the Treasury for the King to grant the benefit of her husband's forfeiture to a third party in trust for herself and her children. He protested this on the grounds that he was, himself, already a significant creditor of the Estate.[*]

The Kilsyth estate was to made a brief appearance in the 1745 rebellion when Bonnie Prince Charlie spent the night at Colzium House on his march to attack Stirling Castle.[†] He demanded the best that Daniel's steward could provide and, when asked for payment the following morning, the Prince refused, saying that 'old Shawfield' could consider he was paying his rent.

The Dangers of Travel

Travelling to and from London to Scotland may seem a fairly straightforward proposition today, but in the early eighteenth century it was still a significant and often dangerous undertaking, as is related by Wodrow in 1730 (although he states that the incident concerning 'Shaufield and his lady' had occurred some years earlier).[‡] Evidently Daniel and his wife, together with Sir James Campbell of Auchinleck, were driving to London in the winter. Travel by coach during this season on the roads of England was almost impossible and only undertaken as a matter of necessity. Their route took them through Boroughbridge in Yorkshire where there was a bridge which frequently became impassible in times of flood. Two or three nights before the Campbells drove through, a 'Popish' lady who lived on a hill nearby, dreamed that she looked out of the window in the night and 'sau a coach, with a lady in it, almost lost ... and that she sent doun her servants and saved them'. The impression made on the lady by this dream remained so strong that the following night she sent her servants to watch the bridge. Nothing happened on the first or following night, but on the third night Lady Shawfield came,

> and, of a suddain, the coach was overturnedd and filled with watter. The coachman got upon one of the horses, to save his life. The good and religious Lady Shaufeild was for some time under watte; with much difficulty, the cocch and lady in it we got out of the watter. Everybody thought the Lady Shaufeild was dead; her body was full of the watter and she was laid on a declivity on the ground till she voided some of the watter, and recovered her senses.[§]

A graphically told tale! Lady Shawfield was looked after by the 'Popish' lady whose name we are not told. On subsequent trips to London, often accompanied by kinsman and fellow MP Sir James Campbell, Daniel would stop at the spot and send a servant to enquire how the lady did.

[*] Calendar of Treasury Papers, CCXXXIV, 1722.
[†] Miller, *The History of Cumbernauld and Kilsyth: A selection of Scottish Forfeited Estate*, p. 28.
[‡] Wodrow, *Analecta*, p. 171.
[§] *Ibid.*

Robert Campbell—the Swedish Connection

As mentioned above, Daniel's younger half-brother Robert settled in Stockholm, establishing himself in the front rank of successful merchants. Robert shipped bar iron, timber and tar to the Clyde in return for tobacco; many of his dealings were with Daniel. We even know that he lived at 79 Stora Nygatan in what is now part of Stockholm's 'old town'.[*] Robert was offered Swedish nationality but he refused despite the fact that by the middle of the eighteenth century, the Swedes had made foreign trade very difficult for non-Swedish nationals by imposing heavy taxes on all goods not carried in Swedish 'bottoms'. He is also recorded as the part owner of a marble mine, Marmorbruket, at Kolmarden in the Ostergotland region of Sweden. He was to become a close friend of a Colin Campbell from Edinburgh.[†] This man had suffered severe financial losses in the South Sea Bubble crash and had fled abroad to escape his creditors. He eventually ended up in Sweden and sailed with the Swedish East India Company leaving us a fascinating record of his trip to China.[‡] Colin bequeathed Robert a mourning ring in his will.

Robert married Magdalena Bedoire in 1713.[§] She was the daughter of wigmaker Jean Bedoire the elder, and sister to Frans Bedoire who helped to promote the Swedish East India company. Her possessions are listed in the Svea Hovratt archive (EIXb, vol. 70) in Riksarkivet, a 26-page document which leads one to assume she was a wealthy young lady. Robert became a person of considerable standing in his adopted country, appointed head of the National Board of Trade late in life and recognised as being 'of the nobility' owing to his mother having been born a Stewart of Bute. He died of tuberculosis at the age of 77 and was buried in the Maria church in Stockholm in the family grave of the Bedoire family. The couple had at least nine children. One son was called Daniel; he was evidently also a merchant and served as Supercargo in Swedish East Indiamen.[¶] A Campbell pedigree shows two of Robert's sons at school in Glasgow in 1725 but they are not named. Since two of the children were called after their uncles, Matthew and Daniel, the boys were probably sent to Glasgow under their supervision. Robert had clearly not forgotten his roots, despite his long sojourn overseas.

Recently two armorial plates have come to light in Sweden; one has Robert's arms and the other celebrates the marriage of Maria, one of his daughters, to a Swedish nobleman. Painted in 1746 and 1753 respectively, these plates were commissioned by an expatriate Scot living in Sweden to be made and painted in China and shipped back to Europe. They encapsulate

---

[*]   Swedish National Archives DNR RA 42-2006/3115, and John Ashton of Goteborg.
[†]   Possibly a Campbell of Moy.
[‡]   John Ashton, 'A Passage to China. Diary of the Swedish East India Company's first Expedition' to China, 1732-33', private printing.
[§]   In an old Argyll pedigree he is listed as marrying a Mary Campbell in 1717, but this seems to be an error.
[¶]   Some of these details were supplied by the National Archives of Sweden.

Robert Campbell of Stockholm's arms from a Qianlong porcelain plate c.1746 (left) and his daughter's arms from a Qianlong porcelain plate celebrating her marriage in 1752 to Count Cedercreutz (Photographs: Nicholas Bastin)

perfectly the extraordinary times in which Robert and Daniel lived and traded; the ambition and breadth of their business activities seem remarkable for that period.*

---

* Robert and Magdalena's eldest son was also called Robert. He served in the British Army in one of the Household Regiments 'the Queen's Guard'. In 1757, he was sent to Stockholm on a special mission by George II. It is almost certainly thanks to his Swedish background that he was chosen for this mission; he had both family and other connections there and, at the time, Britain had no formal diplomatic relations with Sweden. This was during the Seven Years' War when Sweden was technically an enemy of Britain, having sided with Austria, France, Russia and Spain while Britain supported Prussia and Hanover. France was largely responsible for arming Sweden and funding her army.

There are some interesting dispatches in the National Archives (SP95/103); Robert had, of course, been born in Stockholm but had not been home for 19 years when he was sent on this mission. In the previous year an abortive coup had been hatched by Queen Louisa Ulrika to try and reduce the influence of the Parliament and restore the powers of the monarchy. Robert was deputed to talk with the Prussian minister and to discover whether Sweden might be persuaded to throw in her lot with England on the grounds that it would help Sweden's commercial interests. He was regarded by the Swedish Senate with considerable suspicion since he was brother to Maria, Comtesse Cedercreutz, a woman senator who was a very close friend of the Queen. The Queen, Louisa Ulrika of Prussia, was sister to Frederick the Great, and therefore it is hardly surprising that the 'Caps' as the more socialist party in Sweden was known, distrusted both her, and the Court party or 'Hats', who wished to impose absolute monarchy. Louisa Ulrika was the power behind the throne of her weak husband, Adolphus Frederick, who was virtually no more than a figurehead. The Swedish Parliament was informed by the Swedish legation in London that Robert had been sent to Stockholm on a secret mission to the Court and considered him guilty of '*manigance*' (trickery). Evidently his arrival caused some consternation, but he was initially received at Court. Ultimately, however, his activities and presence were felt to be inappropriate and he failed to succeed in his mission.

He left for England on 23 December having accomplished nothing. Letters of recall had been sent from London but Robert had already left before they reached Stockholm. Whether it had been intended by London that he be officially accredited as British ambassador is hard to establish from the limited number of papers in the National Archives. These papers consist, in the main, of correspondence from Baron L. de Marteville, the French minister, who was keeping a close eye on representatives of 'enemy' governments.

7

The Shawfield Riots

It is impossible to over-emphasise the state of abject poverty which existed throughout the greater part of the Scottish Highlands and a good part of the Lowlands in the early eighteenth century. The Scottish people were loathe to acknowledge that they had benefited in any way from the effect of a Union that many asserted they had been virtually starved into accepting. A true degree of prosperity was not achieved until the latter part of the century. With the seat of government at Westminster and with the King never venturing north of the border, or taking any interest in his northern Kingdom, capital outflow was a serious problem. The amount that flowed south is hard to evaluate, but certainly Scottish merchants and nobles began to buy properties in England and to make investments in the more prosperous south. They also hoped by their presence at Court, to benefit from patronage of the Crown. One prominent example, the Earl of Ilay, a Campbell through and through and brother to the Duke, was born and educated in England, although he was to make his name in Scotland; at one time he was even known as 'the King in Scotland' and he was certainly not alone amongst the Scottish nobility in having been born south of the border. His brother, the 2nd Duke, lived *en prince* in England and his factor was constantly scratching for money from his estates in Scotland to maintain his standard of living. The squeezing of his tenantry made the Duke highly unpopular later in life.

The biggest thorn in the side of the Scots, unsurprisingly, was taxation. The revenue collected by Customs and Excise probably failed even to cover the cost of its administration and, as has already been demonstrated by Daniel's own activities, the system was open to abuse. In his role as Collector for the Port of Glasgow, Daniel certainly feathered his own nest and, in common with most prominent figures, he was regarded with distaste by many:

> Campbell of Shawfield, it must be confessed, makes anything but a handsome figure in the story of Glasgow at that time. From first to last he was self seeking and grasping, never missing a chance to enrich himself at the expense of his constituents and doing little or nothing to support and defend the interests of the city which had honoured him by sending him to Parliament.[*]

---

[*] Eyre Todd, *History of Glasgow*, vol. iii.

Bruce Lenman describes him as, 'almost a parody of a hard-faced, grasping Hanoverian Whig merchant oligarch'.[*]

Few taxes were to prove as provocative or far-reaching as the Malt Tax, introduced in 1725. Extending this unpopular tax from England to Scotland had been attempted in 1713, only to be rapidly dropped when the uproar it occasioned seemed likely to dissolve the new and fragile Union. The status quo was probably maintained because the Scottish Presbyterians, although initially reluctant to accept Union, were loathe to abandon it now that it ensured the existence of their established Church, the independence of the legal system and the rights of the Royal Boroughs to retain their privileges. In 1724, with Scotland contributing almost nothing to Central Government's coffers, the question was once again raised in the House of Commons. A motion was introduced by a Mr Thomas Broderick proposing that in the place of duty on malt in Scotland, duty of 6d should be levied on every barrel of ale. It has been suggested that Daniel came up with this idea but, owing to his position as member for Glasgow Burghs (and that of his brother, John, Member of Parliament for Edinburgh and also the current Provost of that City[†]), it was considered more politic to have the bill introduced by someone else. In a letter to Sir John Clerk, Robert Dundas states that he believed Daniel to be responsible,[‡] although as an ardent Jacobite and no friend of Daniel's, his views should be treated with circumspection. Wodrow, the contemporary chronicler, suggests that Daniel had, in fact, voted against the imposition of the tax.[§] It is now impossible to know the truth, although Wodrow was generally very well informed and was never normally lenient where Daniel Campbell was concerned. The *Journals of the House of Commons* are, unfortunately, unable to confirm or deny the fact, since there were four Campbells in the House at the time and entries do not differentiate between them!

The sum of tax proposed was 6d per barrel of ale, but the Prime Minister, Robert Walpole, perhaps sensing danger, pronounced that the figure was too high and reduced it to 3d. Walpole went on to say that the funds thus raised would go to defray the 10 guineas a week that had been paid to Scottish members since the Union, to cover living expenses in London when Parliament was in session. Mahon wrote that Walpole informed the Scots MPs that their costs must in future come out of Scottish revenue or that they must, 'tie up their stockings with their own garters'.[¶]

From correspondence at the time, it is clear that there were still many Scots anxious to scrap the hated Union and ready for any action that might

---

[*]   Lenman, *Jacobite Risings in Britain, 1689-1746*, pp. 207-8.

[†]   John Campbell was member for Edinburgh 1721-34 and Lord Provost several times including 1725.

[‡]   GD18/3199.

[§]   Wodrow, *Analecta*, p. 211. A surprising statement in view of Wodrow's low opinion of Daniel.

[¶]   NAS RH15/208/2.

make their feelings clear to Government in London. For example, in January 1725 John Forbes, in a letter to his brother the Lord Advocate Duncan Forbes, wrote 'I am glad to hear that the Address for dissolving the Union is thrown out by your Faculty; tho' its well known I was not for it ...'.* (The Forbes brothers were in different camps on this subject.) However, the Government in London seemed blissfully unaware of the furore that might be unleashed by the imposition of the Malt Tax. Obviously it was not going to be popular but the subsequent extent of riot and mayhem was most unusual in Scotland at the time.

Ale was the principal beverage of the masses and the poorest people would suffer most as a result of the Malt Tax. Although the most serious trouble broke out in Glasgow, towns throughout the north were simmering with discontent and we know that the Lord Provost John Campbell (Daniel's brother) in Edinburgh swiftly took steps to protect his city. Provosts of the major burghs were vested with considerable powers and even the military were subject to their orders.

The Shawfield Riots: 23–25 June 1725

Mainly as a result of his former position as 'Tacksman of the Revenue', Daniel Campbell was unpopular in Glasgow;† the windows in his house had been broken in January 1725 owing to his perceived support for the newly imposed tobacco taxes. This had made him highly unpopular with other Glasgow merchants involved with the Chesapeake trade although his business records after 1717 have disappeared, rendering it impossible to confirm whether he was still trading in this commodity by this date.

On 22 June 1725 Daniel left his handsome, newly built Shawfield Mansion on the Trongate, for his country home at Woodhall some eight miles distant. It does not seem likely that his departure was in direct anticipation of violence, as his wife and household servants did not leave until the following day. He was certainly fortunate, as it has been suggested that he might well have been 'dewitted'‡ had he been at home when his house was attacked. Daniel's old foe George Lockhart of Carnwarth claimed that it was Daniel who applied to General Wade in Edinburgh to send soldiers to Glasgow, apparently on 21 June.§ However, one has to think that it would have been extraordinary for him to have left his wife and servants in possible mortal danger if this was the case. There is also no mention of this in Daniel's letter of 1 July to Lord Townshend.¶ That he was responsible for summoning Wade does not appear in any other source, so it is quite likely that it was a rumour spread by

---

* Culloden papers, CVIII, pp. 28, 29, i.e. John Forbes was not pro-Union initially.

† Burton, *History of Scotland*.

‡ Brothers Jan and Cornelius de Witt, *Torn in Pieces by a Mob in Holland in 1672*. See Russell, *Three Generations of Fascinating Women*, p. 164 and Lockhart, *History of Old Glasgow*, p. 973.

§ See text of letter below, p. 72.

¶ Lockhart, *History of Old Glasgow*, p. 961.

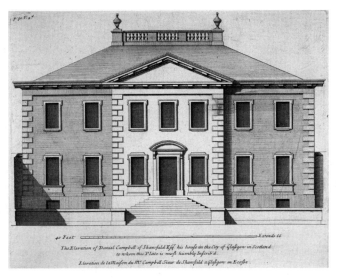

The Shawfield Mansion from Vitruvius Britannicus, *vol ii, by Colen Campbell. (© The British Library Board. All Rights Reserved. Ref 649.b5.)*

Lockhart, ever anxious to discredit Daniel. At the same time though, it seems Daniel must have been aware of trouble brewing; rumours of impending violence were rampant in the town.

A certain John Wodrow is said to have told Hector Thomson, servant to Daniel, that there was a 'flying report that his master's house was to be pulled down and Thomson, having acquainted his Master thereof, returned to Wodrow telling him his master thanked him for his information, but that he already knew of it.[*] John Wodrow was to swear to this on oath before Duncan Forbes, the Lord Advocate, at the inquiry following the riots and the arrest of the magistrates and the Provost. In this knowledge, it is strange that Daniel seems to have taken so few measures to ensure the protection of his house and some of his most valuable possessions. Perhaps he was confident that the troops would arrive in time to prevent serious trouble. On the other hand, it is also a fact that a large number of smaller items such as clothes, linen and silver were saved,[†] but whether Daniel arranged for their removal to the houses of neighbours, or whether well-meaning friends undertook to save what they could in his absence prior to the main attack, is not known. Lists of articles recovered from neighbours after the riots is given in the appendix; there is clothing, household linen and silver; there is no mention of either furniture or paintings.[‡]

[*]   Wodrow, *Avalecta*, pp. 216, 217.
[†]   'Inventory of articles which escaped the hands of the mob on the occasion of the sacking of the Shawfield Mansion in 1725', with notes by J. Dalrymple Duncan in *Transactions of the Glasgow Archaeological Society*, vol XX1V, pp. 368-97. The list is remarkable for the quantity of table napkins!
[‡]   *Culloden Papers*, CIX, p. 79.

The Lord Advocate, Duncan Forbes, wrote to the Magistrates of Glasgow on 25 June that he was amazed that they were unaware of the impending riot, since he heard that it had been much talked about and that the populace was stirred up 'to look upon Mr. Campbell with an evil eye'.[*]

Although Provost Miller swore that he had not sent for General Wade, he did order the guardhouse to be prepared for the reception of two companies of foot soldiers under Captain Francis Bushell. They were expected to arrive on the evening of 24 June. Having done this, he subsequently denied having had any knowledge of impending trouble. Unfortunately, the people who where sent to prepare the guardhouse were set upon by the mob, who took the keys and locked the building. This meant that the soldiers had to be billeted in the town and were thus widely scattered.

There are detailed contemporary descriptions of events on 23-25 June but they do not all agree![†] Nevertheless it seems that on the 23rd a crowd of women and boys appeared in the streets and was dispersed fairly easily having done little damage other than to smash a few windows of the Shawfield Mansion. Events of the 24th were more serious: towards evening a large mob formed and took it into their heads to demolish the house.[‡] It was at this hour that Captain Francis Bushell and his two troops of foot soldiers entered the city only to find that they could not gain access to the Guard House. The men were undoubtedly tired after their long march and the Captain agreed to their being given billets throughout the town, instructing them to lie on their rifles during the night! Scarcely had the soldiers been dispersed than the mob became 'boisterous and directed their fury against Daniel Campbell's house which they gutted and destroyed, pulling down everything that their power could reach to. His gardens destroyed and broke down everything except the walls which it seems they had no leisure to demolish in form.'[§]

Captain Bushell asked the Provost if he should not turn out his men, but Miller, fearing that their presence would prove provocative, resisted. The Provost did, it was reported, move amongst the mob trying to calm them but he failed to read the King's Proclamation—the Riot Act—and on meeting more rioters who threatened him with force, he withdrew. By law, the Riot Act had to be read an hour prior to any 'violence should be done, much less firing sharp shot'.[¶] There was only one other magistrate present at the time— Campbell of Blythswood. Magistrates James Johnson and John Stirling were absent on their own business; did they have advance knowledge which led

---

[*] In Wodrow, *Analectica*; Culloden Papers; *Memoirs of Sir Robert Walpole*; *History of Glasgow* and more.

[†] Lord Advocate to John Scrope suggests that Dundas was one of the chief protagonists in stirring the mob. Robert Dundas of Arniston, MP for Edinburgh, was a former Lord Advocate dismissed by Walpole.

[‡] Culloden Papers, CX, p. 80.

[§] Lockhart, *Old Glasgow*, pp. 958-65.

[¶] Culloden Papers, CXV p. 87.

them to make themselves scarce? The youngest magistrate, Baillie Mitchell, Dean of Guild and by trade a maltster (putting him in the position of being 'responsible for the care of the Tradesmen and Artificers'') was evidently in his own house at the start of the riot. When he was informed of the trouble, he was too frightened to 'venture himself into the Tumult and, though otherwise abundantly capable of his office as a Magistrate, yet he is very unfit for Adventures of that kind'.[†] Patently he was of little use. Later, the Lord Advocate's inquiry revealed that Mr Mitchell had stayed home all day on the 25th and had then slipped out of the city by boat as soon as he had either seen or heard of the destruction of Daniel's house. This was despite being aware of the danger in which the civil status of the city stood and, furthermore, without taking leave of the Chief Magistrate or making any effort to assist in the preservation of the peace. This was accounted a gross Malversation in Office.

On the 25th it could be seen that the house had been virtually demolished— quite an undertaking and hardly the casual violence of a spontaneous mob, but suggestive of something altogether more organised. The rioters were now less violent but many were drunk, having helped themselves to the contents of Daniel's cellar. Millar ordered the guard room broken open and 'pretended further to act so far in his duty as to seize some of the rioters and to commit them to Gaol'.[‡] A man dressed in woman's clothes (some dispute arose afterwards as to whether it was, in fact, a woman) seized hold of a drum and, followed by some boys, began to beat it around the street rallying more and more people. The rapidly growing crowd then marched on the Guard House and attacked the soldiers with stones.[§] The men had little choice but to respond or to flee the city. Captain Bushell commanded his men to fire using powder only, hoping to frighten the crowd into dispersing but, when this failed, they were ordered to 'fire sharp'. Inevitably, tragedy struck. Some activists in the crowd were killed and, it appears, two or three casual onlookers were also either killed or wounded. The generally accepted tally of casualties is nine killed and 17 wounded. The alarm bell was rung; the city's magazine was broken into by people looking for means by which to attack the soldiers. The Provost sent word to Bushell that he should withdraw immediately for his safety. He did so, heading for Dumbarton Castle.

That the Provost was ignorant and cowardly is probable; he certainly handled the affair ineptly and to try and cover his inaction; he professed neither to know nor recognise any members of the mob. It even transpired that he had had a copy of the Riot Act declaration in his pocket during the first wave of trouble, but was dissuaded from reading it from fear of the mob.

---

[*] Lockhart, *Old Glasgow*, pp. 967, 968.
[†] *Culloden Papers*, CXV, p. 87.
[‡] Wodrow, *Analecta*.
[§] Lockhart's account, p. 974.

Retribution

Regiments of dragoons of Lord Stair and Colonel Campbell together with five companies from Berwick duly arrived 'hoping to strike terror into the mutineers in the West and to support the Civil Magistrates in taking up the offenders ...';* the Lord Advocate, Duncan Forbes, added 'the Provost's conduct seems to have as much the airs of guilt as anyones—and yet I am told even by Daniel Campbell himself, that he suspects him of no guilt but only of plain stupidity'. On 9 July the Lord Advocate and General Wade marched their troops straight into the town. Needless to say, there was no sign of disturbance in the face of such a strong force. Mr Forbes immediately began to take statements and to interview witnesses. He had already sent two young men into the town as spies to uncover information about the guilty parties. The Lord Advocate was a very powerful figure and a faithful servant to the Crown during the leadership of Walpole. He had risen to power initially through the influence of the 2nd Duke of Argyll and, together with the Earl of Islay, was largely responsible for ruling Scotland during the governments of Walpole 1725-37. During the investigation and subsequent trial, Wodrow described his bearing as surly and rude (although it is worth remembering that Wodrow deeply disliked Forbes).

The Lord Advocate's letters to London made it clear that he intended to arrest the Provost on grounds of 'Malversation' in respect of his office. Such an action was thought likely to 'strike terror in all the Neighbouring Magistrates who have a disposition to be remiss in their duty'.† A reply from John Scrope in London agreed to the proposals put forward by Forbes and General Wade and further expressed sorrow at the news of 'Mr. Campbel's Misfortune'. Charles Delahaye, Cabinet Secretary to the King, sent a long letter of commiseration from the Lords Justice in London.‡ He added that an account of the affair had been forwarded to the King in Hanover. Daniel received many letters of sympathy, including one from George I, together with promises of compensation, from the Lord Townshend (brother in law to Sir Robert Walpole)§ and from Walpole himself.

Even before the arrival of the Lord Advocate in Glasgow, an account of the riots was published by the *Caledonian Mercury*, a Jacobite newspaper in Edinburgh. The account was strongly critical of the actions (or inaction) of the Glasgow magistrates, impugning to them 'gross insinuations of their being accessories to all the disorders'.¶ The Glasgow magistrates immediately responded with their version of events, which they sent to be inserted in the 'Currant' (*Courant?*), but their counterparts in Edinburgh banned the newspaper from publishing the article on pain of imprisonment. The

---

* Culloden papers, CXIII, Lord Advocate to Charles Delahaye, 8 July 1725.
† Culloden CXIII, p. 82.
‡ NAS, RH15/208/2, letter from Delahaye.
§ NAS RH15/208/2, letter from Townshend in Hanover.
¶ Lockhart, *Old Glasgow*, p. 963.

Glaswegians were furious at what they considered to be a libel against them and a restraint on liberty by refusing them the right of reply.[*]

In a letter dated 1 July 1725, presumably addressed to Lord Townshend, Daniel describes the events of the riots from his perspective:

> I am sorry that the unaccountable fury and mischeif of the town in Scotland in favour of which I have given my friends so much trouble upon a great many occasions, should now oblige me to entertain your lordship with the account of the barbarity with which they have at last used me.
>
> I believe your Lordship is no stranger to the villainous calumneys with which a party in the town of Glasgow supported by the countenance of the people then in power in Scotland persecuted me all last year as if I had been the destroyer of their trade, for no other reason but by the wise method of your brother Walpole took in settling the affairs of the Customs here, there was in a ... an end put their extravagant ... in the tobacco trade (this might suggest, but does not totally confirm, that Daniel was no longer dealing in tobacco himself). Their unjust clamour upon this head so far prevailed that at Michaelmas last they got the government of the town wrested out of the hands of my friends into their own.
>
> I should have been able very soon to have retrieved this ... if new forgerys had not been trumped up upon me during the last session of parliament particularly that from the controversy of the malt tax; and my enemys had no ... a voucher ... then a letter of Mr. Dundas, at that time His Majesty's Advocate
>
> As your lordship knows I am as sensible as any body of the reluctance with which this country would be brought to submit to the malt tax, yet I own I was very sensible we were used with great ... in having but a half imposed on us which England paid the whole.[†] On my return I explained my self in these terms to the magistrates of Glasgow when they came to consult with me what to do in relation to the tax.
>
> I continued in town for three weeks where I was [caressed] by people of all ranks, and being luckily for me obliged to go to a little country seat[‡] I have eight miles from Glasgow on the 22nd, I left them I really thought very well disposed to give obedience to the law.
>
> But to my very great surprise on the 24 about 2 o'clock in the morning a messenger from Glasgow disturbed me with the news that the night before a very numerous mob had broke into my house there, which with great care and expence I had made a very pretty one; robbed me of all my jewels, plate and ready money, and of all the linnens, cloaths and furniture they imagined would be of use to them, as for my glasses, chairs, tables, cabinets, bedsteads and other ... furniture they broke to pieces; my papers, bonds, bills they tore; and about the time the first messenger came off they had broke into my cellars which were but too well stocked for such monstrous guests.

---

[*]   Eyre Todd, *History of Glasgow*, p. 301.

[†]   Under terms of the Union, Scotland was excused from paying some taxes owing to its relative poverty.

[‡]   Woodhall, Lanark—hardly a little place!

I remained at Woodhall all that day distressed with one account after another of the barbarous manner they were proceeding which amounted to this that after gutting my house of everything that was loose, they broke down the wainscotting, pulled up some of the floors, and uncovered the roof of it. They made the same havock in my garden by breaking my statues, pulling up my trees shrubs and hedges by the roots and breaking down two pavilions in it and having received repeated entreaties from my friends begging me to get to a place of safety, I came hither [Edinburgh][*] on the 26th my wife and I stripped of every on thing in the world but the clouth on our backs ... Your Lordship will ... imagine so heavy a misfortune cannot sit easily upon me but I do assure you the consciousness that I have suffered innocently for doing my duty to his Majesty and to my country affords me very great support of mind[†]

Daniel's letter finishes by saying that the mood of Edinburgh appears to be well managed by the magistrates (his brother John was Lord Provost) and that he thinks a word of thanks for their loyalty would, in his humble opinion, be merited.

A few pieces of jewellery, including a diamond, were later recovered. These were offered for sale to a goldsmith, Robert Luke, in the city. Presumably his suspicions were raised by the quality of the goods which were being offered and he informed the magistrates. Further inquiry revealed that the pieces had been bought from a very poor man called William Turnbull who, on being questioned, would not disclose how he had come by them. His house was searched and some further pieces were discovered. They were said to have been taken from Shawfield by his 13-year-old son. Turnbull and the man to whom he had sold the pieces were both imprisoned.[‡]

John Campbell, brother to Daniel and Provost of Edinburgh at the time, wrote to Robert Walpole on 31 July.[§] He describes the 'present temper of the people of Glasgow from whence all the ferment took its rise, is a very odd one'. He describes what happened when Wade and Forbes began their investigation: 'they found some people who condemned the mob; but they found a combination [conspiracy?] among the citizens to conceal the actors and they found nobody in authority there had been at the least pains to make discoverys'. He was further enraged by the fact that the arrival in Edinburgh of the prisoners and the numerous following crowd had inspired the local brewers to go on strike and not to 'brew one drop' until the tax was revoked.

Forbes' first act had been to commit 19 people to prison. On 16 July he issued a warrant for the arrest of Millar, Baillies John Stirling, James Johns(t) on and James Mitchell, Dean of Guild John Stark and Deacon Convener John Armour all 'or complicity in the riots'. Each was denied bail and on 17 July

---

[*]   He had a house, 12 St Andrews Square, in Edinburgh.
[†]   Public Records Office, Treasury Papers, 173.
[‡]   In the account of the riots from a gentleman of Edinburgh to a friend in the country.
[§]   Coxe, *Diaries of Sir Robert Walpole*, p. 410.

they were escorted to Edinburgh together with the Magistrates and Provost of Glasgow. They are said to have been imprisoned, with much grumbling, in the common jail. When the Lord Advocate was asked how the City of Glasgow was to be governed when the magistrates were imprisoned, he said 'there was no fear of dispeace when the heads of the mob were imprisoned'.[*] On 31 July, Provost Miller of Glasgow sent an obsequious letter to King George justifying 'the circumstances of the unhappy disorder'.[†] On 14 August a reply was received from His Majesty's secretary saying that the King was sorry that the Provost and Magistrates' account did not agree with that which he had received from the Lord Advocate.[‡]

Captain Bushell was accused of murder by the magistrates of Glasgow but the Solicitor General threw out the case, to the fury of many people. Bushell was promoted shortly afterwards. When the subject of Daniel's compensation was being discussed in Committee in the House of Commons, Bushell was called as a witness.[§]

There can be no doubt whatsoever from reading a great deal of correspondence, that Scotland was the Government's greatest worry at this time 'as being the chief objects of men's thoughts and conversation'. While the brewers of Edinburgh, Scotland's main city, did not work, discontent increased amongst the people who relied on ale as one of their few pleasures; meanwhile, the Government received no revenue. John Campbell lays much of the blame for the brewers' refusal to work squarely on Robert Dundas: 'the miserable state of the brewers is to be pitied since all efforts to get them back to work had been in vain; they had given themselves up to Mr. Dundas body and soul'. Robert Dundas, later to inherit the title of Lord Arniston, came from a family of distinguished advocates. He had become Lord Advocate in 1720 and was much involved in Scottish affairs; he had lost his position to Duncan Forbes of Culloden when Walpole came to power. John Campbell ends this letter to the Prime Minister with the words 'we [in Edinburgh] are on guard as much as we can be but while this firebrand [Dundas] continues among us, it is hard to say it will always be so'.[¶] Eventually, Forbes, aided by Islay, forced the brewers to go back to work by dint of the Court of Sessions declaring that the strike was illegal. The Duke of Roxburghe was dismissed from his office as Secretary of State for Scotland for his failure to support the Government over the Malt Tax. The Earl of Islay, writing to Sir Robert Walpole on 27 August 1725, said that the brewers' decision to give up their 'strike' had also been helped by drink being brought in from outside, where it had been warmly welcomed by the citizens of the city. Islay was to become known as 'the King in Scotland' and Daniel Campbell was said to 'have the greatest power with Walpole of any Scots man, at least commoner'.

[*]   Wodrow, *Analecta*, p. 217.
[†]   Culloden papers, CXVIII, p. 91.
[‡]   Brown, *History of Glasgow*, p. 303.
[§]   House of Commons Journal, 1725, pp. 600, 601, 620, 624, 625, 626, 689.
[¶]   Coxe, *Diaries of Sir Robert Walpole*, Campbell to Walpole, 31 July 1725, pp. 440, 441.

The trial of members of the Glasgow mob opened in the Justiciary Court in Edinburgh. It was something of a farce. Of the 'mob' that were on trial only one man and one woman from the first 10 prisoners to be tried were found guilty. They were sentenced to perpetual banishment; the other eight were absolved of any blame. Five others were sentenced to transportation for complicity. They were shipped aboard the sloop *Princess May* whose skipper, Captain Simons, wrote a letter dated 1 December 1725 '... having on board five of the Glasgow rioters, a Corporal and five men of the Rt Hon. My Lord Deloraine's Regiment to guard ...'. The men were named.* The rest of the prisoners who were found guilty were sentenced to be 'whipped through the streets of Glasgow[†].

There was considerable uproar at the idea that the Lord Advocate, himself a Justice of the Peace, took upon himself the authority to put his fellow Justices on trial; it was almost certainly illegal. In the event, the magistrates did not face trial.

Restitution

Daniel had received a letter, dated 16 July 1725, from Lord Townshend acknowledging receipt of his 'account of the great misfortune which had befallen you by the violent rage of the mob at Glasgow'.[‡] He added that he had laid the letter before the King 'who was much concerned at your suffering and ordered me to let you know that you should not be a loser by what has come upon you on account of your loyalty to him and your zeal for the service of his government'.

Daniel was encouraged to petition the House of Commons setting out his losses and asking for compensation. This request, made in the first half of 1726, was strongly backed by the chief Government officers, the Argyll faction and Walpole himself. Both Houses passed the Bill and awarded him the sum of £6,080 for the destruction of his house and nearly £3,000 for the loss of his possessions. Concerned that they would have to bear the cost of Shawfield's damages (rightly as it turned out), the City of Glasgow submitted an estimate from Baillie Ramsay and a Mr Graham, a tradesman, for repair and restoration of the Shawfield Mansion. A quote of between £300 and £400 was submitted to Parliament, but 'Mr. Walpole and his influence in the House was too strong for them and all was concluded as Shawfield would have it'.[§] It would seem unlikely that all the damage described above could possibly have been made good for such a relatively modest sum (all these figures were enormous for their day) but most people felt that Daniel had come out of it pretty handsomely.

---

*   SP Domestic, Geo. 1, bundle 59, no 54; bundle 60, no. 1.
†   Eyre Todd, *History of Glasgow*, p. 302.
‡   NAS, RH15/208/2.
§   Wodrow, *Analecta*, p. 314.

The Master of the Rolls insisted that the damages should be met by Glasgow. By the time the case was heard in London, George Drummond had succeeded Daniel's elder brother, John Campbell, as Lord Provost of Edinburgh. Drummond was called as a witness. He said that he had frequently been in the petitioner's house which 'was about 60 foot in front, and 48 foot in depth, built all of Freestone'; that most of the rooms were wainscoted and finely furnished; and that he 'verily believed, the Damage which is done to the House and Gardens only, cannot be repaired for £2,000 Sterling.'* His account was confirmed by other witnesses and they all insisted that the fine furnishings, pictures, silk beds and other rich furniture could not possibly have been purchased for as little as the £1,500 that the Petitioner was claiming. Drummond, Alexander McMillan and James Nimmo together with 'Mr. Campbell Junior'[†] all gave evidence to the effect that Daniel Campbell always had a large sum of money in his house in his 'scrutoir'. This seems plausible in an age when coin was scarce and notes barely existed. Then there was the jewellery. Another witness, Mrs Sommervell, the 'Petitioner's Lady's Woman' declared she had seen the jewellery frequently; that her lady kept it in 'a fine strong box in her Closet; and always left them there when she at any time went into the country ...'. She was very sure

> ... the said strong box was in the House on the 24th of June last, when it was robbed; for that after hearing of the Mischief that had been done to her Master's house, she went into Glasgow on the 25th of June about Eight in the Morning; and went through all the House, while a great many of the Mob were in it; and at that time, she saw this strong Box and her Master's Scrutoir lying broke and empty in one of the Rooms.

The same witness described the jewellery in some detail.[‡]

George Drummond's account of 'Discussion in the House of Commons, upon the Application of Daniel Campbell, esq., of Shawfield, for compensation for his losses by the riot in Glasgow' was addressed to the Hon James Erskine of Grange. A copy was sent to the Rev Robert Wodrow[§] who jotted some figures on the back of the letter. These were:

To Shawfield house and gardens	2,000
Loss in furniture	1,500
In money and bank notes[¶]	1,640
In gold and medals of Miss Campbell	200
	6,080

---

* House of Commons Journal, 1725, p. 624.
† Possibly his son, John.
‡ House of Commons Journal, 1725, p. 625.
§ *Miscellany of the Abbotswood Club*, vol. 1, p. 419.
¶ Banknotes were still very rare at the time; these may have been largely promissory notes.

So where was the money going to come from? It was reported, probably via rumours disseminated by Daniel's friends, that he 'would rather have another house pulled down than have recourse to Glasgow for relief'. He certainly needed to distance himself from any degree of responsibility for the enormous sum of nearly £10,000 to be borne by the city; he was, after all, Member of Parliament for the burghs and hoping to be re-elected in the forthcoming elections. Be that as it may, on 26 April 1726 it was agreed to raise the money through the 'imposition of an extra 2 penies Scots upon all Ale and Beer brewed and sold in the City of Glasgow and Privileges thereof for satisfying the Damages and Losses which Daniel Campbell Esquire lately suffered in a riot there ...'.[*]

Daniel's inveterate enemy Lockhart is, of course, sceptical as to the true value of compensation due:

> there is all the reason imaginable to believe it could not possibly amount to the 6th part of it; for as he [Campbell] was threatened and did expect what happened, it is not to be imagined that when he retired into the Country with his wife and family, but he would likewise take the money, jewels, banknotes and plate which he pretended to lose ... whereas the outward fabric (as the law directs in such cases) was repaired at the public expense of the Town and a great part of the furniture was saved or recovered so that the wainscotting ... and a few scrub figures called statues in the Court were only destroyed.[†]

The description of the 'few scrub figures called statues' must have annoyed Daniel. Lockhart continued even more censoriously, 'but the Ministers were resolved to do something to purpose towards gratifying their Creature ...'.

The true figure, perhaps, lay somewhere in between, but if Lockhart can castigate Daniel for knowing he was going to be attacked, it is yet another reason for suspecting deliberate negligence on the part of the Provost and the absent magistrates who were never brought to trial. What is a fact, is that a very handsome mansion, possibly Scotland's finest early eighteenth-century building, and one designed by another Scot, was virtually destroyed.

Daniel chose not to rebuild his once impressive house, electing instead to sell the remains to Colonel William McDowall, formerly a successful merchant in the West Indies. He had married the daughter of a rich plantation owner in St Kitts and returned to live in Glasgow. He paid £1,785 for the battered shell and set about rebuilding it. He added two wings 'built forward' to the line of the Trongate (the easternmost of the wings stood for many years after the house itself was gone).

The enduring grandeur and architectural importance of the Shawfield Mansion can be seen from the fact that Bonnie Prince Charlie spent Christmas

---

[*] House of Commons Journal, 1725, p. 689.
[†] Lockhart, *Old Glasgow*, p. 975.

there in 1745 after his retreat from Derby. He simply commandeered the house, staying for a week. It must have rendered Colonel McDowall apoplectic since he was a staunch Hanoverian. The Prince gave balls and dinners, but it is said that he was shunned by loyal Glasgow society and his only guests were a few local Jacobites. An interesting footnote is that while he was staying in the Shawfield Mansion, the Prince met and fell in love with Clementina Walkinshaw, the daughter of John Walkinshaw of Barrowfield, a formerly rich merchant but staunch Jacobite whose estate had been amongst those forfeited after the '15. (Daniel had had many financial dealings with Walkinshaw.) Following the Prince's return to France, he sent for her and she became his mistress. Exiled from France, where Charles Edward's activities had become an embarrassment, the couple were living in Liège, Belgium when their daughter, Charlotte, was born in 1753.*

Following McDowall's death in 1748, the house was eventually sold for 1,700 guineas to another well-known merchant and one of Glasgow's richest citizens, John Glassford, once again emphasising its long-standing position as the grandest address in Glasgow. It is said to have been John Glassford's favourite house. The building was later sold by his son for £9,850 and was pulled down in 1780 to open up the street which is now known as Great Glassford Street.

The Shawfield Riots were arguably the most serious civil commotion in eighteenth-century Scotland; the uproar probably exceeded even the Porteous Riots in Edinburgh 10 years later. When considering their impact, it is worth taking into account the febrile state of the Hanoverian regime at that time. After all, the Government was anxious and watchful for an attempt to unseat them in favour of the Stuart pretender. Scotland was always the focus of their concerns, as it contained many active Jacobites, as well as a large number of skilled and effective men at arms, in the shape of the irregular highland soldiers that the disaffected Clan Chiefs could call upon. The armed uprisings of 1715 and 1719 reinforced Hanoverian fears that Scotland was not to be trusted; and the riots, which on close examination were rather too organised to be simply the popular outpouring of frustration by the people of Glasgow, were directed against the Hanoverian regime's most visible and high profile resident in that city. The riots would have been interpreted by the Government, rightly or wrongly, as striking a direct blow against the King's interests. There is no firm evidence that it was explicitly motivated by Jacobites, although they would doubtless have relished Daniel's losses, and there are other parties that could also have played a role. Tobacco merchants, for example, resented paying tax on their goods—a tax they perceived as being

---

* Charlotte had a long and well-hidden affair with Prince Ferdinand de Rohan, Archbishop of Bordeaux, by whom she had three children. A descendant of her daughter, Marie Victoire, lives today in Poland.

the result of Daniel's efforts at Westminster*—and were most upset that the Chesapeake trade was going to be seriously affected. Daniel certainly felt that it was his role in helping Walpole to bring the tobacco trade under the control of Customs which was the real cause and directly stated this in his letter to Lord Townshend following the riot.

As we have seen, Daniel had his fair share of critics and enemies. Some, such as Lockhart of Carnwarth, an ardent Jacobite who had despised him since his arrival in Glasgow on the coat tails of Argyll, spared no opportunity to make capital out of Daniel's hardships. In Lockhart's own account he proposes that the riot and the subsequent events were in some part a settling of old scores with Daniel, since the previous Michaelmas' election had

> undermined and turned out Campbell's friends who had enhanced the Government for many years; and being some of them, particularly Provost Aird [the previous Provost of Glasgow] under pay, were mere tools to him; and this was thought a proper Occasion to Squeeze them and, if possible, to replace Campbell's set.†

Both Daniel and his enemies, therefore, saw the riots as being part of a deeper plot against him, caused by his role as the principal Hanoverian 'fixer' and supporter in Glasgow. Rather incomprehensibly, neither party seemed to ascribe the cause of the riot exclusively to the imposition of the Malt Tax, although this was certainly the catalyst. What seems certain is that, although there was widely held popular anger at the imposition of a new tax on malt, the channelling of this anger towards Daniel satisfied the interests of a good number of his enemies, many of whom disliked the Hanoverian monarchy and Union with England. That the Government responded so swiftly and robustly in his defence and with such generous compensation, sent a further powerful message to both its supporters and its enemies.

Whatever the truth of it, the Government had a chance to show the cities of Scotland that it would not tolerate a breakdown in law and order. It was extremely concerned that memories of the serious rebellion in 1715, the less well-known and ultimately almost farcical uprising in 1719 (which most worryingly for the Hanoverians included 500 professional Spanish soldiers), and the so-called Atterbury Plot of 1722, were still fresh in people's memories. Jacobites were often a convenient scapegoat. The bursting of the South Sea Bubble was sometimes attributed to the Jacobites along the lines that if there was a major disaster, some blame must surely lie with them!

The destruction of Daniel's fine home did present him with one positive outcome: the compensation he received was sufficient to enable him to complete the purchase of his last great estate, that of the Isle of Islay.

---

*   This would appear to suggest that he no longer traded in tobacco.
†   Lockhart's account, p. 974.

8

Laird of Islay

T
he island of Islay lies at the extreme southern end of the inner Hebridean chain. It sits some thirty miles off Kintyre in Argyll and the same distance from the northern tip of Ireland. Described as the 'Queen of the Isles' and the 'Green Island', Islay has always been considerably more fertile than most of the other islands off the West Coast of Scotland and it also contains assets in its mineral deposits, slate beds and peat bogs. The coastline is made up of steep and rugged cliffs coupled with wide sandy beaches and large areas of white dunes. Slate is found in the northern part of the island and approximately ten per cent of the surface ground is covered by the peat bogs.

Port Askaig, a small hamlet on the west coast, sits at the narrowest point of the Sound of Islay which separates this island from that of Jura. This neck of water is notoriously dangerous but this did not prevent cattle, one of Islay's major exports, being forced to swim across the sound. The beasts were often shod with horse shoes for the long drive across Jura to Laggan and from there to the market in Falkirk and frequently even further, to England.

In Dr Margaret Storrie's *Islay, Biography of an Island* she writes:

> An island of considerable character and contrasts, one of the few Hebridean islands with woodlands, one with a wild and bare west, a tidy central heartland and a fragmented south-east, Islay's distinctiveness is in part a reflection of its physical setting and structure. To a much greater extent it is the result of a history very different from that of the remainder of the Hebrides and the Highlands. More particularly it reflects the perception and initiative of relatively few individuals during a century or more after about 1750 ...*

One might well imagine that Islay's very situation led to complete isolation, but during the domination of the Lords of the Isles, whose headquarters had been at Finlaggan on the island in the fourteenth and fifteenth centuries, it was a political and cultural centre for the west of Scotland, probably due to the fact that most essential travel was undertaken by sea. During the next period though, travel difficulties—prior to General Wade's road building programme in the Highlands and the eventual introduction of ferry services—did lead to a

---

* *Islay, Biography of an Island*, pp. 24, 25.

considerable degree of separation from the mainland and events in the rest of Scotland often had little impact on life in these islands. This began to change with the arrival of the Campbells of Cawdor (fellow clansmen and distant kinsmen of Great Daniel) in 1615.

The arrival of these Campbells in Islay signalled the end of the Clan Donald's long reign; they did not leave quietly. Initially regarded as unpopular interlopers the Cawdor Campbells gradually brought a degree of stability to Islay and Jura, helping to integrate the islands into Scotland. At the start of their incumbency, the Campbells found that their rent roll yielded a good return, but by 1651 this had shrunk to only one-tenth of the original income. Prices remained low and successive years brought short bursts of feast interspersed with long periods of famine. The island's isolation did, however, ensure that it largely escaped the civil and religious strife affecting the mainland.

In 1688, Sir Hugh Campbell of Cawdor gave the island to his son, Alexander, but the latter predeceased his father and the next heir was Alexander's son, John. This young man inherited in 1716 and found that his legacy was something of a poisoned chalice; bad harvests and virtual famine had rendered the tenants unable to pay their rent and many of them were on the verge of starvation. Descriptions of contemporary life can be found in the Anderson papers.[*] James Anderson and his son, Patrick, were both writers for the *Signet* in Edinburgh and handled the Cawdor Campbell's business affairs. It is said that Sir Hugh took some interest in his island property but Alexander was seldom there and when John inherited, Islay's affairs were in a very sorry state.[†] Letters in the Anderson papers include the comments '... there is not one cow out of Islay ... not 30 are drovable ... there is no money in the country just now'. This is particularly striking given the relative fertility of the land, showing the poor state that Islay had been reduced to through neglect. It certainly compares unfavourably with the 2,800 black cattle worth over £4,700 that would be exported 44 years later.[‡] Patrick Anderson told John Campbell of Cawdor that there was no chance of obtaining a mortgage from any bank since the estate was already heavily encumbered by debt. Young John was evidently something of a spendthrift and it seems that his other estates meant more to him than the rather barren island of Islay which yielded only a net annual income of £755 at that time.

In 1723 John Campbell met Daniel, probably in London. In common with some other prominent Glasgow merchants, Daniel was a sort of one-man merchant bank. He advanced money to John Campbell,[§] possibly in the

---

[*] James Anderson papers, NLS, Advocates MS. 29.1.2.

[†] Patrick Anderson, 1719. He was a writer to the *Signet* in Edinburgh and apparently acted as a financial agent/advisor for John Campbell of Cawdor.

[‡] Figure from Dr John Walker's report on the Hebrides, quoted in McGeachy *Argyll 1730-1850*, pp. 45-6.

[§] In the absence of banks as we know them today, goldsmiths offered much the same services.

knowledge that he would be in line for eventual acquisition of the whole of Islay; one can be sure that Daniel was well aware of young John's poor financial situation. Daniel proposed a deal that involved his advancing the capital sum of £6,000 to run for 21 years together with a payment of £500 per annum. In return for this 'wadset' or lease, Daniel had the sole right to the management of the island of Islay together with a large part of Jura, and their revenue until the wadset was redeemed.[*]

Accounts of resistance to John Campbell of Calder show his tenants in Islay to be far from pliant:

> the most stubborn among them, which consists of those who have the very best and most improveable possessions doun of [below] the rent, do ridicule all we have done and resolve to defend themselves if any removals be insisted upon ... I hope Shawfield will either come himself or send one in whom he can put entire confidence and who may be acquainted with the people; and then he shall know who are his friends most to be trusted, and who are otherwise affected. For we are divided and turn'd into pollitick factions, that it's hard to trust to many. I am heartily pleas'd it has fallen in the hands of so good a friend of our own as Shawfield, and one who is capable to improve the countrey and keep the people under right government, and make them understand themselves of late.[†]

It is an interesting to consider why Daniel might have been intent on purchasing Islay, since at the time it could hardly be seen as a profitable venture. While it may simply have been that he could not resist a bargain, Daniel was also supposed to have had Islay connections through his mother, Jean Campbell of Ballmeanach, although it is difficult to know what these may have been. In any event, Daniel seemed anxious to ensure that he had a serious base in Campbell territory and he does not appear to have ever had any interest in investing in property in England or the Lowlands, which might have made more commercial sense. If it was clanship and a love for the rugged and demanding countryside, it must have been one of the few occasions when his heart overruled his head.

In 1726, following the Shawfield Riots in Glasgow, Daniel was awarded over £9,000 in compensation. John Campbell of Cawdor was unable to redeem his bond, and Daniel completed the purchase of Islay using this compensation to make payment of a further £6,000. Thus the total cost of purchasing the Island of Islay, together with nearly half of Jura, cost him the total sum of only £12,000. The Anderson lawyers in Edinburgh were unhappy that their principal, John Campbell, had disposed of this asset without due

---

[*] Jupp, *The History of Islay*, p. 129.

[†] Letter from George Campbell of Octomore to Archibald Campbell, the lawyer to Campbell of Calder from G.G. Smith. *The Book of Islay*, pp. 426-9 and quoted in McGeachy's *Argyll 1730-1850*, p. 82.

consultation;* Great Daniel was not known as 'the canny Scot' for nothing! After 120 years the reign of the Campbells of Cawdor was over and that of the Campbells of Shawfield was beginning. This branch of the Clan was to prove much more 'hands on' than its predecessors.

There is a suggestion that the Duke of Argyll had, himself, asked Daniel for his opinion on the possible purchase of Islay and that Daniel had advised against it. The truth is that the cost was more than the Duke could afford at the time and Daniel was delighted to pursue the acquisition on his own account. He was also probably still annoyed with the Duke, who had failed to support his candidacy for the seat of Glasgow Burghs in the 1715 parliamentary elections.

Lamont in his *Early History of Islay* writes: 'There is a sense in which the history of Islay as we know it today, begins with the purchase of the Island by the Campbells of Shawfield in 1726.'†

Great Daniel—still known as 'Shawfield' but soon to be of 'Shawfield and Islay'—was the first 'improver' of Islay. After all, he had not made his fortune without a shrewdness that led him to expect a return on his investments. He possibly decided to spend more of his time and energies on his new acquisition and he gave his estate of Shawfield to his eldest son, John.‡ On Islay Daniel began to initiate improvements and his grandson, Daniel the Younger, writing in 1777, said that from the time his grandfather acquired the estate,

> He immediately began and zealously carried on, extensive plans for the improvement and civilization of that corner. Every encouragement to Agriculture as the basis of his own and of his tenants prosperity, was his great Object. To the branch of the flax husbandry and manufacture he particularly turned his care and attention. He laid out in building Lint Milns, bringing to the Island, Manufacturers, Hecklers, Weavers etc. considerably above £2,000 sterling.§

One of Daniel's more important contributions to Islay was the expansion of the Stent Committee's rights and responsibilities. The Stent Committee, established by John Campbell of Cawdor, was a sort of local parliament or council composed of the 'gentlemen and feuars, heretors and tacksmen'. It was responsible for payment of teachers and doctors, and the maintenance of the churches, amongst other things. It was through the Stent Committee that Great Daniel can also be credited with establishing the first post office at Kilarrow in 1744. Three runners were employed to carry the mail from Islay to other parts of the island and to Inveraray—the latter route followed that of the ancient drovers from Port Askaig across the sound of Islay, across Jura to

---

* Cawdor papers, bundle 657.
† Lamont, *Early History of Islay*.
‡ This property is not to be confused with the Shawfield Mansion in the Trongate of Glasgow itself.
§ NAS E727/60; E728/47; E727/60/1.

Laggan and then again by boat to Keills. This was a long and tiring journey, and one which may well have been unique at the time.[*]

Daniel was a founding member of the Hon. Society of Improvers in the Knowledge of Agriculture, set up in 1725, and he tried his best to ensure that his own Home Farm was an example to the islanders of that society's aspirations. In addition, he was to introduce new industries such as the cultivation of flax and the weaving of linen.

From 1730 many of the tacksmen chose to emigrate to the New World. The colony in New York had advertised for Protestant immigrants and around 450 people are known to have left Islay at the time. Scotland has always 'exported' its talented individuals and this could be seen as one of many periods where intelligent and ambitious men left to try a new life.[†] The exodus was led by Captain Lachlan Campbell, who was to build himself a house, apparently very grand by the colonial standards of the day, in Orange County, New York. The house was called Campbell Hall. Some of the tacksmen who left did so because they were unhappy with the new fixed-term leases being granted under Great Daniel's regime; they were afraid of being the losers under this new order.

Daniel's initiatives were part of the wider transformation of the Highlands, which was evolving from a feudal existence into the modern world. This would later be evidenced in the Highland Clearances, as chiefs and landlords sought to take greater control of 'their' land. Daniel was no chieftain and could have expected none of the obligations that tacksmen would in the past have provided in return for their holding of the land. It is no surprise, therefore, that he would have sought to regularise tenancies and, although there is no suggestion that he 'cleared' these tenants, they demonstrably felt that their future might be brighter in America rather than face the uncertainty of staying on the island under a new landlord.

The approximate population of Islay in the 1730s appears to have been around 5,500 but from 1755, when it stood at 8,364, it rose steeply until, by 1831 it totalled 15,000. Much of this increase can be laid at the door of improved agricultural methods, the introduction of new crops such as potatoes, improved healthcare and the establishment of the famous distilleries. Today the population is some 3,500: a comment on the changing times.

Thanks to its position at the head of Loch Indaal, Bowmore was chosen as the first 'model' village on the island. Daniel the Younger created the village and the inhabitants of Kilarrow moved there in 1768. The reason for this has been said to be largely due to his desire to enlarge the gardens of Islay House which had been impossible due to the presence of the village of Kilarrow. Bowmore was well sited and its harbour meant that small ships could sail

---

[*] Clifford Jupp suggests this in *The History of Islay*, p. 139.

[†] As opposed to the generally held theory that it was mainly criminals who were 'exported'.

Islay House (Photograph: Nicholas Bastin)

right up to the quay on the high tides all the year round while larger vessels of up to 300 tonnes could anchor offshore.* Whisky distilleries were to be set up after Great Daniel's death; the first, Bowmore, was founded in 1779. This industry was to become very important in respect of tax revenue raised for the Government; for example, it amounted to some £30,000 in 1835 despite an allegedly lax customs regime. Some of the most widely known whiskies in the world are acknowledged to be the malts of Islay: Ardbeg, Lagavulin and Laphroaig being amongst them.

The smaller island of Jura was far less productive than Islay. The name 'Jura' comes from the Norse for 'deer' and there are still around 6,000 red deer who share the island with about 200 two-legged inhabitants. In 1739, Daniel feued his stake in the island back to his baillie there and this family became known as the Campbells of Jura. The rest of the island was in the possession of the Macleans of Lochbuy.

Daniel was to be Laird of Islay for 27 years and, despite the fact that he was MP for Glasgow Burghs when he first completed the purchase, he appears to have spent several months each year on the island. In 1731 he added flanking wings to Islay House (formerly known as Kilarrow House) which lies at the head of Loch Indaal. Such an expenditure would suggest that he spent enough time on the island with his growing family to make the additions worthwhile. The original building, constructed in the time of Sir Hugh Campbell of Cawdor, had been a simple tower house.

---

* Pennant, *A Tour in Scotland and a Voyage to the Hebrides.*

We know little of the remainder of Daniel's life. During the 1745 he reappears to play a minor role that reflects his upbringing and antecedents, and demonstrates that, despite the veneer of eighteenth-century enlightenment, one did not have to scratch too deeply to reveal the clansman beneath. In response to the arrival of Bonnie Prince Charlie who, as we have seen, had the temerity to commandeer his old house in Glasgow and subsequently stayed at one of his houses at Kilsyth, he acted as any self-respecting tacksman would and roused out his men to fight and defend the land. He is described in a letter from Major General John Campbell of Mamore (later the 4th Duke of Argyll):

> Shawfield has not only brought a fine body of men from Islay but has given them belts and other necessaries, and in short tho' he knows the value of money has been most lavish of it on this occaision in fitting out his men. He has been of the utmost service to me in regulating the extravagent demands of others ... I wish the Duke of Argyll would drope him a line of thanks. He deserves it and wants nothing for himselfe or family.[*]

It is typical of his upbringing that Daniel would turn out his men to fight in such a situation. He clearly viewed his military role as a responsibility, just as his father and grandfather and their fathers before them, and although he was obviously far too old to fight himself, he took the trouble to equip his company to a high standard. It is ironic that this action, which in its own small way helped to contribute to the extinguishing of the clan system, was borne out of that very mindset.

His eldest son and heir, John, also played an active part in the '45 melee, fighting with the Argyll militia, doubtless commanding the company of men raised from Islay. He wrote a description of the battle of Falkirk in which the rebels triumphed in one of the last successful highland charges in history and crushed the Government forces:

> 'Tis morally certain that our generals on Friday were far from expecting a battle and consequently were caught unprepared in manie circumstances, among which none of the smallest were quartering the Argyllshire corp in places both at such a distance from the camp and from one another that it was impossible to assemble them in time, especially as no post in the army had been. assigned to them ... It was such a hurricane both of wind and rain blowing hard quite in the face of our army that I could hardly sit my horse ... I hate talking big on these occasions we have had enough of that before the battle and I shall never think it safe to despise an enemy hereafter.

He lost his horse, his baggage and his servant during the course of the battle and was doubtless lucky to escape otherwise unscathed.

---

[*] Mamore MS 104/5/8 quoted in Sir James Fergusson, *Argyll in the '45*, pp. 59-60.

John died the following year on 22 July, at Kilsyth, leaving his eldest son, Daniel, usually referred to as 'Daniel the Younger', as the heir to Great Daniel.

Great Daniel had other military connections that came to the fore at the time of the '45: his nephew Colin, the son of his elder half-brother Angus, had inherited the family seat, the castle of Skipness in Kintyre. He married Daniel's daughter Anne, his first cousin, making him both son-in-law and nephew to Daniel. Colin was a successful soldier and had an eventful career; he was described 'as a very sencible man and bred an officer'.* He played an active role in the early Highland Regiments and in 1725 he was commissioned as Acting Captain of one of the independent Highland companies. These were known as 'Am Freiceadan Dubh' (the Black Watch) after the government tartan that they wore and which has come to form the basis for many clan tartans including that of Clan Campbell. These independent companies were the forerunners of all the famous Highland Regiments. It was the first time that a Government had kept a standing army in Scotland. Up until this date, all militias had been irregular troops, disbanded as soon as their immediate task had been fulfilled. In 1739, Colin was posted as captain and employed on duty in Argyll and Lochaber. His role largely involved watching the Stewarts of Appin and the Clan Cameron who were heavily involved in cattle rustling and extortion in the area. Thanks to the scale of these illegal enterprises, it was no easy task to exert any control since the clansmen travelled deep into the Lowlands to lift the herds of cattle before driving them into the hills where they were easily hidden.

Colin was active in the search for Bonnie Prince Charlie in 1746—a quest which Daniel must doubtless have wholeheartedly approved—and is said to have been within three miles of the Prince on the island of Uist. He was in command of Mingary Castle in 1746 at the time when the rebels were being disarmed and handing in their weapons. On 26 May Colin wrote 'this day the Laird of Glencoe brought me in some arms from his clan in this country, viz. thirteen firelocks, six very bad swords, one holster piston, one dirk ... I expect more arms tomorrow'. This type of haul, which seems to have been typical, was not very convincing coming as it did from such an active clan. Colin also writes that most of the arms were evidently king's arms and there were few highland pistols or broadswords. In other words he was merely recovering a few well-worn weapons that had previously been stolen from the army.

Colin also had a role in one of the Highlands' most infamous escapades; the murder of Campbell of Glenure, 'the red fox'. The murderer was thought to have been Allen Breac Stewart, aided by James Stewart of the Glen. (Robert Louis Stevenson was to turn this story into *Kidnapped* and *Catriona*.) At the trial, Colin was Chancellor of the Jury and, therefore, responsible for delivering

---

* Cambell of Mamore MS, M537 and quoted in Sir James Fergusson's *Argyll in the '45*, Faber and Faber, 1961, p. 82.

The 'Shawfield' Mazer and charger given to Bothwell parish church on Daniel's death (Photograph: Nicholas Bastin)

the guilty verdict after a trial that had lasted for 48 hours without a break. James was hanged, although it was generally accepted that he was not the murderer. Stewart escaped with his life and probably moved to France.

There exists an amusing anecdote which probably concerned Colin's wife, Daniel's daughter, Anne. In common with many of this branch of the Campbells, even today, she was both tall and 'large', standing over six feet tall. She became known as 'Big Lady Anne of Skipness'. The story goes that one day she passed a group of workmen at Skipness who were involved in repairing the castle's massive entrance door. Seven of them had managed to remove the door but could not replace it. Lady Anne ordered them to get out of the way, picked up the door and replaced it, single-handed, on its hinges!*

Colin died in 1756, leaving no children, and the Skipness estate reverted to his cousin Daniel the Younger of Shawfield and Islay.

We know little more of Great Daniel, except that he died at the principal family home of Woodhall on 8 June 1753 and that his funeral was held on 15 June in the ancient church of Bothwell, bordering the estate. The location of his tomb is a mystery. A family vault perhaps lies under what is now the choir because we know that many other family members were interred at Bothwell, including Robert of Skipness in 1814.[†] The only visible memorials are plaques to Daniel's son Walter and Walter's wife, Elinor Kerr, both of which are almost completely hidden by the organ. It is just possible that the great man himself did not wish to have an opulent tomb, but it is more probable that the entrance to the mausoleum could have been moved or destroyed when what is now the choir of the church was opened up to form part of the main body of the church.[‡]

Bothwell has a silver mazer and charger made by silversmith Robert Gordon of Edinburgh in 1756. These were given to the church following Daniel's death, inscribed with his name and the date of his death. They are still in regular use at baptisms.

---

* Graham, *Skipness, Memories of an Highland Estate*, pp. 42-4.
† Robert's wife, Eugenia Wynne, put up a plaque in his memory at Skipness in which she says that his ashes lie far away at Bothwell.
‡ Bothwell church was originally built against the medieval chancel of an earlier building.

9

Great Daniel's Descendants

Daniel the Younger, 2nd of Shawfield and Islay (1737-1777)

Daniel the Younger was 16 when his grandfather died in 1753. Described as a man of great sweetness of character and significant intelligence, he enjoyed the high life and where his grandfather had amassed a huge fortune, this young man only equalled him in the rate at which he spent it. He kept a pack of hounds, led a lavish life in London and travelled extensively. He was also highly cultured and interested in music, being an above average violinist. Young Daniel was evidently a most attractive man, with much charm, and he was sometimes known as 'the long love' in reference to his height—a trait he had clearly inherited from his grandfather.

As a young man he did the Grand Tour, in the course of which he collected a wide range of objects and paintings. He also met the glamorous and well-known Russian, Princess Ekaterina Romanova Daschkow. This meeting led to a long and close friendship, perhaps more than mere friendship, which lasted until his death. The Princess was living in Edinburgh when he died. A remarkable woman, she was a daughter of Count Roman Worontzow, born in 1740 and married at 15 to Prince Mikail Daschkow. She became a close friend and confidant of the Empress Catherine and is said to have been prominently involved in the murder of the Emperor Peter.[*] Widowed young, the Princess took a journey through Europe and it was in Aix en Provence that she met Daniel. They travelled together to Montpelier and Marseille before engaging two river boats and, together with quite a large entourage, making a trip down the Rhine. They also visited Geneva where they had several meetings with Voltaire; Daniel acquired several sketches of him done by the artist member of the party, M. Hubert. They eventually parted at Spa. Five years later the Princess arrived in Edinburgh with her son who was to study history under Professor Robertson at Edinburgh University. She evidently took rooms in Holyrood House and remained in residence throughout her son's studies. She saw a great deal of Daniel both in Edinburgh and at Woodhall. On one of her visits to Woodhall, Daniel gave her the 'famous Shawfield pearls' and she responded with a portrait of herself. Could this be the portrait of an unidentified lady, lot no. 79 in the Sale Catalogue of 1854? The Princess

---

[*] Russell, *Three Generations of Fascinating Women*, pp. 170-4.

wrote in her memoirs that these years were the 'most satisfactory and happy of my life'.

Young Daniel was elected in 1760 as the representative for Lanarkshire with the support of the Dukes of Hamilton, Argyll and Douglas and Robert Dundas of Arniston, but he failed to secure re-election in 1768.[*] The presence of the Duke of Hamilton amongst his supporters demonstrates how far relations between the families had improved since Great Daniel's day! The Duchess of Argyll replied to a letter of William Mure saying 'What shall I say to Shawfield if he comes this way?; I think the boroughs[†] (Lanark, Linlithgow, etc.) might be offered to him. He was once too high and mighty to accept of such an offer and he may be so yet, but if they could keep him out of the county, I think it would be worthwhile'. Either he was, indeed, too grand to accept this sort of demotion or he was not offered it, since he was not re-elected.

While he was demonstrably extravagant, Daniel was also both educated and enlightened, and the island of Islay had much to be grateful for during Young Daniel's lairdship. He founded the now world famous village of Bowmore, site of the first legal whisky distillery on the island; it was swiftly followed by several other distilleries. The illegal distillation of whisky was also common on the island at this time as, indeed, it had been for centuries. *Uisge-beatha* or *acquae vitae* had been brought to Scotland from Ireland as early as the fifteenth century. The raw materials were plentiful and all were found locally: barley, peat and the 'right' sort of water. Needless to say, the Church of Scotland deplored this industry, especially since, at the time, no excise duty was paid. In the Statistical Account of Scotland in 1794 it reported that 'we have not an excise officer in the whole island'.

Bowmore church, built in 1767, is of an unusual circular construction, romantically said to be so that the devil could not find a corner to hide in. The truth is that, thriftily for once, Daniel the Younger had borrowed some plans originally drawn up for his kinsman, the Duke of Argyll, which were intended for the church in the new town at Inveraray, but which were subsequently replaced by the design for the church that stands there today.

Bowmore was one of the first 'planned' villages to be built in Scotland. Daniel applied several times to the Annexed Estates Commissioners for financial aid to develop various industries in the islands. His first memorandum to them, was probably too broad in its range of demands and was turned down,[‡] but subsequent applications proved successful. His philanthropy is evident in that he always agreed to match whatever sum the commissioners might award with his own money. He also pointed out to them that his grandfather, Great Daniel, had already spent great sums of money on agricultural and fishery improvements during his lifetime. His requests to the commissioners

---

* The Duchess of Argyll wrote to William Mure: Caldwell Papers, ii(2) 223.
† As opposed to the Shire which he been representing.
‡ Annexed papers in the NAS E727/60 series.

included a ferry service, the church for Bowmore, a schoolhouse and salary for the schoolmaster, and a contribution towards the development of linen manufacture and the fishing industry. He also wanted to build a prison!

He was not content to leave Islay House as he had inherited it, adding two stair towers and an octagonal east tower in 1760.[*] By now the house looked very grand with large elegant windows replacing the original narrower openings typical of tower houses. It also had a fashionable Georgian interior. Quite why he felt it necessary to make these additions when he was, and would remain, a bachelor, is perhaps just another example of his many extravagances.

During Young Daniel's lairdship, there is mention of mining activities on Islay. Some mining had been going on for years, perhaps since even the times of the Viking settlements. In 1770 eight mines were in production. There were also deposits of lead ore, copper and a small quantity of silver. A handsome silver goblet of Islay silver made by Adam Graham in 1780 can be seen in Glasgow Museum. Young Daniel commissioned a report on the possibilities of improving and developing the mining industry. This report concluded that a profit could be made but Daniel, with his knowledge of the more extensive mines in Lanarkshire, around his home at Woodhall for example, was never very enthusiastic.

By Daniel's death on 12 May 1777, he had set the island on a solid path of development; his lairdship had been imaginative, generous and, for the times, humanitarian. Unfortunately it had also been expensive and although he had bought the freehold of the Kilsyth estate for £22,800 in 1772 and promptly sold it the following year to Sir Archibald Edmonstone for £41,000, he died deeply in debt. Kilsyth was the first of many properties which had to be sold.

Walter Campbell, 3rd of Shawfield and Islay (1741-1816)

Daniel the Younger was succeeded by his younger brother Walter (1741-1816). Walter married Eleanor Kerr in 1768; they had 11 children. His second wife was Mary Nisbet of Direleton, with whom he had three more. Of his eight female children only three left descendants: Harriet married Daniel Hamilton;[†] Margaret married Francis, 8th Earl of Wemyss; Katherine married Sir Charles Jenkinson, 10th Bt.

Walter very swiftly discovered that, in addition to inheriting the vast estates acquired by his grandfather, he had inherited the debts amassed by the extravagances of his elder brother; these amounted to approximately £90,000.[‡] There was a pressing need to raise some cash. The first piece of the estate that he sold was that of Shawfield in 1788 when the first financial cracks were appearing in the family's finances. In order to do this and to break the act of entail, the family had to apply to Parliament. He also sold those parts of the

---

[*]   Forman, *Islay House*; RCAHMS, Argyll Inventory, vol. v, p. 294.
[†]   The Family of Lord Hamilton of Dalzell were her descendants.
[‡]   More than £8 million today.

island of Jura that Daniel had acquired together with Islay back in 1727,[*] but managed to consolidate the family holdings on Islay by purchasing the last outstanding estate—that which was known as Sunderland in Islay. The sale of Jura was to lead to several cases being brought against the Islay Campbells a few years later. This was because the cattle droves had crossed the island to Laggan for at least a hundred years, probably much longer. Now new roads had been built on Jura but Archibald Campbell, a descendant of the family's former baillie on the island, tried to ensure that the cattle from Islay did not use these new roads but kept to the old, much slower hill routes.

Despite the efforts already made by Walter's elder brother, Islay afforded no protection against the famines of the 1780s and '90s. With the dawn of the industrial revolution, young men began to drift away from the island, drawn by the new manufactories on the mainland that required their labour. In 1794, the Minister of the Kirk in Kildalton observed that 'the females are more numerous than the males, a great number having left the parish and gone to the Low Countries [the Lowlands of Scotland] for employment ...'.

One of Walter's more imaginative notions was he 'with his unwonted activity and beneficience, built a brew house ...'. In 1808, J. MacDonald had made his own acquaintance with Bowmore and had already approved the strong ale as having 'a laudable change in the taste of the whisky drinking classes on that island [Islay] many of whom now prefer good ale to bad whiskey and have relinquished the detestable habits of drunkenness in which they were formerly too apt to indulge'![†]

The difficulties in which the island found itself were greatly exacerbated by the conclusion of the Napoleonic Wars. Thousands of soldiers, who had helped to defeat the Corsican's armies, now returned home to find themselves without the means to make a living. The new freedom for the international trade which had been all but impossible during the Continental Blockade of the Napoleonic era, now led to the price for grain and other commodities being severely depressed, with imports from America successfully undercutting the British prices. The kelp industry, which had played a significant role in Islay, where it was burned to produce potash for the glass industry, collapsed, as foreign supplies could be obtained more cheaply.

Walter spent much of his life trying to improve his lands in Islay. He introduced many agricultural reforms, built bridges and roads but by the time of his death, agricultural prices in Scotland were, once again, very hard hit. Unfortunately, the combination of all of his philanthropic activities with the misleadingly rosy outlook for agricultural prices during the Napoleonic Wars, led to him spend far in excess of what the estates could bear. His

---

[*] He retained the rights to hunt in the deer forests of Jura and this privilege was also extended to the Duke of Argyll (GD641).

[†] MacDonald, *General View of the Agriculture of the Hebrides or Western Islands of Scotland*, Edinburgh, 1811, p. 630.

death left a still greater burden of debt his upon successor, his grandson, Walter Frederick.

Walter died in 1816 and is buried in the circular church of Bowmore in Islay.

Walter's Sons

During his lifetime Walter, with great wisdom, distributed family property to each of his sons.[*] The eldest, John (1770-1809), would have inherited Islay and Woodhall, but for the fact that he died before his father. John had married Lady Charlotte Campbell, daughter of the 5th Duke of Argyll, and they had two sons and six daughters before his early death. Lady Charlotte was a noted society beauty and many of her friends thought she had thrown herself away on a handsome face. John Campbell was evidently yet another very tall Campbell of whom it was written:

> When Campbell walks the street
> The paviours cry
> 'God bless your legs!'
> And lay their rammers by

John was a soldier and served in the Guards, rising to the rank of Captain before leaving the army in about 1799. The couple lived for a few years at Hartwell House, Buckinghamshire, better known as the home in exile of Louis XVIII (known as 'Louis dix huitres' for his gluttonous habits). After leaving the army, John served in the Argyll militia, and was Colonel at the time of his death. He was also briefly Member of Parliament for the Ayr Burghs between 1807 and his death in 1809. Lady Charlotte became a lady-in-waiting to the Princess of Wales[†] and is the reputed authoress of the *Diary Illustrative of the Times of George IV*, published in 1838. She also married the children's tutor, the Rev. Edward John Bury, which caused a great scandal at the time. One of John and Charlotte's daughters was given the name of Harriet Beaujolais Campbell. She acquired this curious middle name at the request of her godfather, Louis Charles d'Orleans, Comte de Beaujolais and brother to Louis Philippe; she was always known as 'Beaujolois'. There are many mentions of the Comte de Beaujolais staying with John's brother, Robert and his wife, Eugenia Wynne[‡] at Skipness.

Walter's fourth son, Robert, was given Skipness.[§] Most of what we know about him comes through the diaries of his wife, Eugenia Wynne, and her sisters Betsey Fremantle[¶] and Harriet Hamilton.[**] These diaries portray a vivid

---

[*]   Son Daniel had drowned in the Clyde.
[†]   Caroline, the unstable and unfortunate wife of the Prince Regent, later George IV.
[‡]   Fremantle, *Journals of Elisabeth Wynne*, vol. 3. (Also known as the Wynne Diaries.)
[§]   Robert was given Skipness on the occasion of his marriage to Eugenia Wynne in 1806.
[¶]   Betsey married William Fremantle whose accounts of the Navy in the Napoleonic Wars make interesting reading in his wife's diaries. He ended his career as a Rear Admiral.
[**] Fremantle, *The Wynne Diaries*.

picture of social life in both London,* the grand houses of England, such as Stowe (home of the Grenvilles), and in Scotland. It is the only really personal description we have of these Campbells and the manner in which they lived. They evidently moved in the top layer of society. For details of their affairs we can look, for example, at the betrothal of Eugenia. At the end of April 1806, she wrote 'Mr Campbell paid me a long visit this morning—I believe I can guess why he calls so often? ...'. On the 30th, following an outing together to the rehearsal of an opera, Robert asked her if he could call the following morning. The next day he proposed 'in the handsomest and most honourable manner and with all the feeling of a Man who is sincere'. Eugenia was thrown into great agitation. She felt she barely knew him and he told her that he only had an allowance of £1,000 a year from his father and that he would not marry until he had found some sort of employment. He was thinking of abandoning the law and trying to find an appointment as political secretary to a politician. Sister Betsey wrote in her diary for the same day:

> a very handsome proposal made with much candour, honesty and tender-ness—Eugenia already seems to like him excessively ... but unfortunately he is only the second son, dependant on his father who has £25,000 a year [this, as we know, was not really accurate]. The eldest brother [John] has married Lord Lorne's sister.†

In any event the young couple married at the end of the year. They had two services. The first was a very quiet, almost secret, Roman Catholic mass at Twickenham.‡ Robert's brother, Walter of Sunderland in Islay, was his supporter. They had barely time for breakfast and for Eugenia to put on her bridal dress, before they assembled for the second wedding. Following this service the party repaired to Argyle House where the bridal pair was showered with gifts, including a very handsome amethyst and diamond cross from the Comte de Beaujolais. The couple appear to have been idyllically happy together and they spent much of their married life in what sister Betsey described as the wilds of Scotland. We have a description of one of their journeys to Skipness and Islay. On 22 August they embarked from Liverpool on their journey. The seas were very rough '... the Sea rose Mountains high'. Eugenia describes her first impressions of the island. The view from Islay House being quite beautiful and

> although destitute of trees seems to lay claim to a high degree of picturesque beauty—I am diverted by the Sight of barefooted and barelegged poor

---

* Through the Wynne diaries we hear much family gossip, since the other Campbells in London included Robert's younger brother Walter and their sister Katherine who had married Charles Jenkinson, later to inherit his father's Baronetage. Katherine's marriage produced a long line of eminent descendants from Princes of Prussia, Ducs de Montebello, Dukes of Grafton, the families of Normanby, Yarborough, Iveagh (Guiness) and so on.
† The Lady Charlotte Campbell, daughter of the 5th Duke of Argyll.
‡ Eugenia Wynne was a Roman Catholic.

people who enjoy themselves much thus unencumbered with too much attire ... I am an object of great curiosity to the inhabitants with whom, Robert seems a great favourite ...

In September they finally made a long planned expedition to the island of Jura. The crossing was again very rough and they took two hours to reach the Jura shore, 'a truly wild country'. The Comte de Beaujolais, one of their guests, was evidently a keen sportsman and is mentioned as having gone over to Jura many times on his own and being successful in the number of deer he shot. There are accounts of other visits to Jura to hunt the red deer and of trips by boat—often through very rough seas—to visit relations and friends.

Robert died in Glasgow in 1814—'his death was occasioned in consequence of a fall which he had met with ten years ago, and which produced a tumour on the brain'.[*] He left three children, including another Walter who was to be the last Campbell to live at Skipness. Eugenia erected a memorial to Robert in the graveyard of the Kilbrennan Chapel at Skipness although he was buried at Bothwell in the family crypt.

Even after Walter's death in 1816, enlightened division of the family estates continued. Walter's second youngest son, also Walter,[†] received the estate of Sunderland in Islay; Colin, the youngest, received Ardpatrick on West Loch Tarbert, overlooking the sea to Islay, which had been purchased in the 1790s from the MacAlistairs of Loup (another set of distant cousins). The Sunderland in Islay estate was subsequently advertised for sale in *The Scotsman* on 22 July 1840. Evidently hit by poor harvests and economic malaise the younger Walter could not make it pay its way either.

Walter, son of Robert, was quite a character. A keen big game hunter, he spent much of his life in India and penned two books: one became a classic—*The Old Forest Ranger*; the other features his Indian memoirs, in which he describes tiger hunting: 'never attack a tiger on foot—if you can help it. There are some cases when you must do so. Then face him like a Briton and kill him if you can; for if you fail to do so he will certainly kill you.'[‡] Lord Archibald Campbell wrote of Walter in his own memoirs 'Skipness was to all of us in boyhood and remained in our manhood, the beau ideal of what a highland chieftain should be ... he was without exception the most picturesque man in our county of Argyll ...'.[§] Unfortunately, despite these attributes, Walter did not make any money, and the Skipness Estate was sold in 1843. At this time the family owned 15,000 acres but were so destitute that they had to live with their neighbours, the Campbells of Auchindarroch. Skipness became yet another casualty of the wider economic and agricultural crisis in the Highlands in the 1840s.

---

[*] Eugenia's entry in the family bible.
[†] Walter married Mary King and had two daughters.
[‡] Quote in Brander, *Big Game Hunters*, p. 24.
[§] Campbell, *Records of Argyll*.

Walter Frederick, 4th of Shawfield and Islay (1798-1855)

Walter Frederick was the eldest son of John and Lady Charlotte and grandson of Walter. He inherited the main estate from his grandfather in 1816. Walter married his first cousin, the Lady Ellinor Charteris, daughter of Francis, 8th Earl of Wemyss, in 1831. Another Campbell 'improver' despite an unstable financial situation, Walter Frederick did his best; he built several more model villages: on Islay the first was Port Ellen named after his first wife; a second, Port Charlotte after his mother Lady Charlotte Campbell, and a third Port Wemyss, after his father-in-law. The construction of these new villages provided much needed employment and also served to concentrate the population in more urban settings thereby freeing up land to be cultivated in larger strips.* Life in the islands was not easy during these years and the potato blight that arrived from Ireland in the 1840s was a catastrophe. It was first discovered in a field near Port Ellen and within the year had spread throughout the island.

Walter Frederick sat for Argyllshire in four Parliaments where he supported Catholic Emancipation and the Reform Bill—two major pieces of legislation at the time. *The Scotsman* recorded an electioneering visit he made to Campbeltown in Kintyre in January 1836 where he was royally entertained. The article concluded:

> There is but one sentiment in this district as to Mr. Campbell of Islay. He has proved himself the true and staunch supporter of all our local interests, and he is like those who have gone before him, a firm friend both to Church and State. We have not seen the young man who is to oppose him. No man need come to oppose Islay in Kintyre.[†]

Doubtless Walter Frederick's heart was in the right place, but he had little idea of management and had inherited an estate already heavily in debt. His improvements, though important, were too expensive for the estate to bear in a time of agricultural crisis. He had hoped to manage his affairs without recourse to the Treasury, but famine overwhelmed the island and he was left with little alternative.

With no money coming in, it seems rather bizarre that Walter Frederick chose to extend Islay House. He employed a well-known Victorian architect, William Playfair, in the early 1840s to make further additions which were described as 'offices'. It may be that his true motive for undertaking this construction was to provide local employment. Islay House had now become one of the largest houses in the Hebridean islands with some 365 windows and 24 bedrooms.

In 1848, Walter Frederick's long battle to keep his estates and to provide for the *ileachs*, his people, came to a sad end. The banks foreclosed and the

---

* Some might consider this 'clearance' but the rehousing would seem to negate this idea.
† *The Scotsman*, 16 January 1836.

Walter Frederick Campbell and Lady Ellinor landing on Islay, painted by George Sanders (Photograph courtesy of the Scottish Portrait Gallery; painting property of Francis David, 12th Earl of Wemyss and March, K.T)

estates of Islay and Woodhall were sequestrated, with his debts estimated to stand at around £815,000—about £49 million today. 1847 had been a year of national financial crisis and Walter Frederick was in 'good' company when his bankruptcy was gazetted on 5 January 1848.

John Ramsay, who was to purchase part of the Islay estate, paid some handsome compliments to Walter Frederick many years later. In November 1883, Ramsay and his wife entertained 'the tenantry and others resident on the property and gentlemen connected with Islay' to celebrate his 50 years on the island. At the dinner, he made a long speech describing the island when he had first arrived:

> I remember well when I first landed in Islay, the people lived in a quiet and secluded way—quiet because they were very poor and secluded they were then, as they are now, shut off from the rest of Scotland by that narrow strip of sea ...*

He went on to say that there was no regular steam communication between the mainland and the island and few roads and bridges on the island itself.

---

* *The Scotsman*, 29 November 1883.

He recounted how communication had been established by the enterprise of Lord Macdonald and Walter Frederick Campbell, together with the latter's uncle, Walter Campbell of Sunderland in Islay. He explained that it had been these gentlemen who showed the advantages that might accrue to the West Highlands and islands by improving communications with the mainland. He also referred to Walter Frederick's efforts to improve education and described how he personally helped some islanders emigrate to Canada when they were faced with poverty and near starvation on the island. Ramsay pointed out that in the last years before sequestration, Walter Frederick had received no rent whatsoever; the people had simply had no money at all.

After selling Islay, Walter Frederick Campbell left Scotland and went to live in Avranches in Normandy on the charity of his friends; a sad end to a noble-minded laird. He died in 1855.

John Francis Campbell (1821-1885)

Walter Frederick's heir—though heir to what, one might well ask—was John Francis Campbell (1821-1885). He was known as *Iain Og Ile*—meaning Young John of Islay in Gaelic. The only child of Walter's first marriage to Lady Ellinor, John Francis was devastated when his inheritance was sold off by the creditors and he tried over several years to prove that the mineral rights at Woodhall were worth a great deal more than the amount that had been realised by the sale of the estate.

John Francis Campbell as a boy (Painting property of Francis David, 12th Earl of Wemyss and March, K.T)

John Francis was undoubtedly a very clever man, but one with so many diverse interests that he may have spread his talents too thinly, preventing him from making any great achievement in any one of the many areas that interested him. He is perhaps best known as a Gaelic scholar and for his seminal collection in four volumes of *Tales of the West Highlands*, which pioneered folklore collection techniques. He was given a long obituary in *The Scotsman* on 20 February 1885, describing both the sad circumstances leading up to the forced sale of his inheritance and his life's works. These included considerable travel and scientific and literary pursuits. He was trained as a barrister and served as Private Secretary to the Duke of Argyll when the latter was Lord Privy Seal in 1853. He was appointed a Groom of the Privy Chamber and as 'Groom in Waiting in Ordinary to Queen. Victoria by whom his services were said to be highly appreciated'.[*] An interest in science led to his co-operation with a Mr Stokes to invent an instrument for measuring sunshine: the Campbell-Stokes Sunshine Recorder. These machines can still be found and work extremely efficiently.

John Francis died in Cannes during one of his many travels and is buried there. His grave is marked by the Kildalton Cross with the epitaph 'An eminent scholar, Linguist and Traveller, A true Patriotic Highlander, Loved alike by Peer and Peasant.'

Wishing to record the life of one of its favourite sons, Islay erected a suitable monument to his memory. In 1888 about £300 was raised by subscription and Mr Charles Morrison, whose father had purchased much of the island, made available a site near Islay House. The monument was executed by a sculptor, D. Haggart of Glasgow. It was 30 feet in height and consisted of an obelisk 17 ft long surmounting square columns 13 ft high and 6 ft square at the base. One part of the inscription, much of which is in Gaelic, translates as:

> Young John of Islay, a true Highlander, a real gentleman, and a gifted scholar who won fame and honour in every clime. Although he did not inherit the estate of his forefathers, he inherited the love of Islaymen and his memory will be long lasting among the sons of the Gael.[†]

The original monument was struck by lightning (or possibly just blown down in a strong gale) in 1911; it was replaced with an identical model by the Islay Association.

Dispersal

The estates having been sequestrated in December 1847, the trustees in bankruptcy needed to find purchasers for both the estate of Woodhall, Lanark and Islay, Argyll. The sales were not easy to achieve, despite numerous articles and advertisements extolling their merits.[‡] Scottish property was something of a glut on the market with agricultural prices at rock bottom. Islay was a remote and magical place which offered sporting, fishing, mining and agricultural possibilities. The property for sale covered some 139,000 acres including woodlands and pasture together with shooting and fishing. The rental income was quoted at £19,712[§] (though it was not made obvious that one of the reasons for selling the property, was that no income had been forthcoming

---

[*] Obituary in *The Scotsman*, 20 February 1885.
[†] *The Scotsman*, 2 June 1887.
[‡] *The Scotsman*, 6 September 1848.
[§] The arrears in rent amounted to £32,000 by 1847.

for several years). In addition there were minerals, marble quarries and slate workings; one must not forget, either, the presence of 11 distilleries.

James Morrison of Basildon Park (a distant relative of the Campbells), was one of the richest men in Britain. He paid £451,000 for the estates in 1853.* The parishes of Kildalton and Oa were then sold to John Ramsay, who had already been on the island for some years, and had been in charge of running Walter Frederick's affairs following the laird's departure.

Many of the contents, including some of the family portraits were included in the sale. The Morrisons had little intention of living in Islay House which the son, Charles, described as 'inconveniently large' and with the 'soft furnishings in Islay House being a parcel of old, faded, unfashionable, shabby ... rubbish'.† Poor Walter Frederick, while adding offices to the rear of the house, had obviously not been able to replace his curtains and carpets!

The first sale of family possessions was held by Christies at Woodhall on 3 August 1850, when many paintings attributed to old masters that may have been collected by Daniel the Younger or other members of the family when they did the 'grand tour' were sold, including pictures by Veronese, Albano, Rubens, Domenichino, Caracci, Titian, Spagnoletti, Murillo, Sir Godfrey Kneller and Sir Peter Lely. What they fetched is not recorded. A follow-up sale was held by the Dowells and Lyon auction house in Edinburgh on 29 and 30 November 1854. The sale was titled:

> Superb and valuable service of gold and silver plate weighing upwards of 3,000 ounces, collection of paintings, engravings and sketches of the fine arts; select cellar of choice wines, remarkable painting on lapis lazuli, rare raffaelle ware; old indian and other china; articles of vertu, curiosoties, etc.

It included three fine landscapes with cattle and figures by Rosa di Tivoli, two Bellinis, paintings by Weenix and Campidoglio, *The Martyrdom of St Sebastian* by Marinari, and picture frames by Grinling Gibbons.‡

Woodhall, Lanark, long-time (since 1711) principal home of the Campbells of Shawfield and Islay, proved harder to sell. Even allowing for the depressed economic times, this is difficult to comprehend as it was well located for both Glasgow and Edinburgh. Nonetheless it was still being advertised seven years later in *The Scotsman* in July 1855. The estate was described as consisting of 2,407 acres with 2,142 in arable land, 250 in woodland; the remainder comprised ornamental gardens and parkland. The net rental yield for Woodhall was approximately £11,000 and £17,000 for Islay. The advertisement also described the estate as abounding in 'coal, ironstone

---

* Storrie, *Islay, Biography of an Island*, p. 165.
† *Ibid.*
‡ Auction Catalogue of Dowells & Lyon of property of Walter Frederick Campbell, NLS shelfmark K.R, f.2.

and fireclay extending, it is believed, over the whole property and supposed inexhaustible'.* It was also pointed out that there were extensive quarries and an abundance of clay suitable for the manufacture of bricks and tiles. There was no mention of the handsome mansion house and its extensive gardens. Woodhall survived one fire, at least in part, but a second in 1860 effectively put an end to the mansion as a private house. Woodhall was later bought by Alexander Whitelaw, ancestor of a more recent prominent Tory MP, William Whitelaw. Woodhall was sold by the family's creditors for approximately £170,000. This was no small sum at the time but John Francis Campbell, who should have inherited it, considered it had been virtually given away when the true value of the mineral rights was taken into consideration.

In 1771 an Act of Parliament had been passed approving the construction of the Monkland Canal which ran from the old Monkland Coal works to Glasgow. In 1790 an extension was opened, reaching Woodhall. Eventually the canal fell into disuse and there was no traffic after 1935. Some traces of it are still visible.

The remains of the park were surveyed in 1995 by Historic Scotland in advance of improvements to the M8, which bisects the driveway from the entrance of the estate to the site of the house. This survey was undertaken in order to establish whether there were sufficient remains to affect the planning proposals. Unfortunately, the survey concluded that although the policy woodland areas were still important and that there were areas of interest for possible restoration, such as the lake and the walled garden, there was too little remaining for the park as a whole to be protected and restored.

---

* *The Scotsman*, still advertising Woodhall for sale in July 1855.

10

Epilogue

Rags to Riches to Rags in Three Generations'? It took Great Daniel Campbell's descendants only one more than that to lose everything that had been his legacy to them. By the mid-nineteenth century, little trace remained of the empire he had created

Daniel rose from his birth as the third son of a laird of a relatively minor branch of the great Clan Campbell to a become a figure at the very heart of Scottish affairs. His entry into public life was as a protégé of the Duke of Argyll, but he seized every opportunity that this offered him and eventually 'stood on his oun legges', as Wodrow wrote. He created his own luck; he seized every opportunity.

The fortune he amassed in the course of his long life was enormous for the times. Its foundation was laid by his successful trading activities as a very young man. After all, he had only been aged 20 when he had recognised the advantages of doing business with the North American colonies and the West Indies, despite the obstacles posed by the English Navigation Acts and the wars with France. In the space of only two years he had personally experienced and survived most of the dangers encountered in the trans-Atlantic trade in that era of small boats, roving privateers and enemy navies. He was tough; he had needed to be.

Early on in his life, he understood the importance of property as a financial asset, as collateral for his banking activities, as the outward manifestation of his growing success as a public figure and as evidence of his rising social status. His descendants were to marry into the aristocracy; he put the Campbells of Shawfield and Islay firmly on the social map.

His stays in London as a Scottish Commissioner for the negotiations for the Treaty leading to the Act of Union, introduced him to sophisticated contemporary taste in architecture, painting and furnishings; he wasted no time in commissioning his own mansion and embellishing it as befit a man of rank and fortune. It is a great pity that no trace remains of either of his most interesting houses: Woodhall and the Shawfield Mansion.

We are indebted to the writings of Robert Wodrow and George Erskine, amongst others, who have left a wealth of description covering major events of the period leading into the era of 'Enlightenment'. Although both of these men heartily disliked Daniel Campbell!

Daniel's life bridged the gap between the widespread poverty of the seventeenth century and the newly prosperous times of the real Age of Enlightenment which, most people would consider, began in the mid-eighteenth century with the works of philosopher and historian David Hume, economist Adam Smith and so on. It is certainly not easy to visualise 'pawky' Daniel as a philosopher but he surely would have embraced the tenets attacking dogmatism and, above all, economic restraints.

One interesting question, which can now never be answered, is why Daniel never received a title. Many of his contemporaries were awarded recognition for doing far less for King and Government. Given his connections with the King, at Court and with Walpole, it seems likely that he remained amongst the rank of commoners through his own choice.

A powerful and controversial character, Daniel made many enemies but, as Constance Lady Russell wrote, he was indeed 'a very canny Scot'.*

---

* Russell, *Three Generations of Fascinating Women*, p. 158.

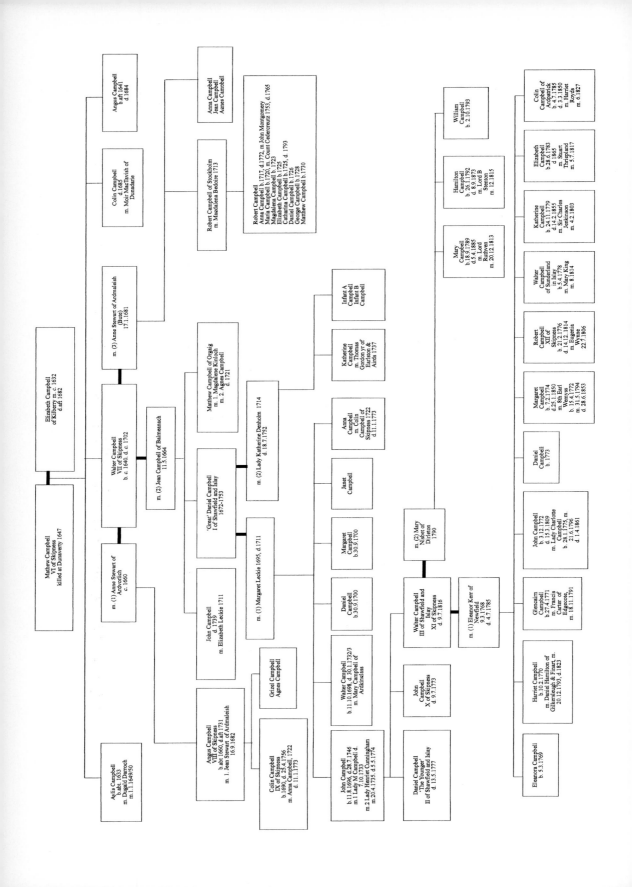

Mathew Campbell VI of Skipness killed at Dunaverty 1647

Elizabeth Campbell of Kilberry m. c. 1652 d. aft 1682

Aylis Campbell b. abt. 1653 m. Dugald Darroch m.1.1.1649/50

m. (1) Anne Stewart of Ardvoirlich c. 1660

m. (2) Jean Campbell of Balmeanach 11.5.1664

m. (3) Anne Stewart of Ardmaleish (Bute) 17.1.1681

Angus Campbell b aft 1641 d. 1684

Colin Campbell d. 1685 m. Mori MacTavish of Dunadene

Walter Campbell VII of Skipness b. c. 1640 d. c. 1702

Anna Campbell Jean Campbell Agnes Campbell

Robert Campbell of Stockholm m. Magdalena Bedsire 1713

Robert Campbell
Anna Campbell b.1717, d.1772, m. John Montgomery
Maria Campbell b.1720, m. Count Cedercreutz 1753, d.1765
Magdalena Campbell b.1723
Elizabeth Campbell b.1725
Catharina Campbell b.1725, d. 1793
Daniel Campbell b.1726
George Campbell b.1728
Matthew Campbell b.1730

John Campbell d. 1739 m. Elizabeth Leckie 1711

Angus Campbell VIII of Skipness b. abt 1660, d. aft 1731 m. 1. Jean Stewart of Ardmaleish 16.9.1682

Matthew Campbell of Orgaig m. 1. Magdalene Kinloch m. 2. Agnes Campbell d. 1721

'Great' Daniel Campbell I of Shawfield and Islay 1672-1753

m. (1) Margaret Leckie 1695, d.1711

m. (2) Lady Katherine Denholm 1714 d. 18.7.1752

Colin Campbell IX of Skipness b.1690, d. 25.4.1756 m. Anna Campbell, 1722 d. 11.1.1773

Grizel Campbell Agnes Campbell

John Campbell b.11.8.1696, d.28.7.1746 m.1 Lady M Campbell d. 7.10.1733 m.2 Lady Henriet Cunningham m.20.4.1735. d.5.5.1774

Walter Campbell b.11.10.1698, d. 30.1.1732/3 m. Mary Campbell of Ardkinglass

Daniel Campbell b.30.9.1700

Margaret Campbell b.30.9.1700

Janet Campbell

Anna Campbell m. Colin Campbell of Skipness 1722 d.11.11.1773

Katherine Campbell m. Thomas Gordon yr of Earlston & Airds 1737

Infant A Campbell Infant B Campbell

Daniel Campbell 'The Younger' II of Shawfield and Islay d. 13.5.1777

John Campbell X of Skipness d. 9.7.1773

Walter Campbell III of Shawfield and Islay XI of Skipness d. 9.7.1816

m. (2) Mary Nisbet of Dirleton 1790

m. (1) Eleanor Kerr of Newfield 9.3.1768 d. 4.7.1785

Eleanora Campbell b. 5.3.1769

Harriet Campbell b.10.2.1770 m. Daniel Hamilton of Gilkerscleugh & Eaart, m. 20.12.1793, d.1823

Glencairn Campbell b.27.4.1771 d. 25.1.1850 m. Francis Carter of Edgecote, m. 18.11.1791

John Campbell b. 3.12.1772 d. 15.3.1809 m. Lady Charlotte Campbell b. 28.1.1775, m. 21.6.1796 d. 1.4.1861

Daniel Campbell b. 1773

Margaret Campbell b. 7.2.1774 d. 25.1.1850 m. 8th Earl Wemyss b. 15.4.1772 m. 31.5.1794 d. 28.6.1853

Robert Campbell XII of Skipness b. 21.2.1776 d. 14.12.1814 m. Eugenia Wynne 22.7.1806

Walter Campbell of Sunderland in Islay b. 5.4.1778 m. Mary King m. 8.1814

Katherine Campbell b. 24.11.1779 d. 14.2.1855 m. Sir Charles Jenkinson m. 4.2.1803

Elizabeth Campbell b.28.6.1783 d. 1865 m. Stuart Threipland m. 5.7.1817

Colin Campbell of Ardpatrick b. 4.7.1785 d. 3.3.1850 m. Harriet Royds m. 6.1827

Mary Campbell b.18.9.1789 d.5.4.1885 m. Lord Ruthven m. 20.12.1813

Hamilton Campbell b. 26.1.1792 d. 8.9.1873 m. Lord B Stenton m. 12.1815

William Campbell b. 2.10.1793

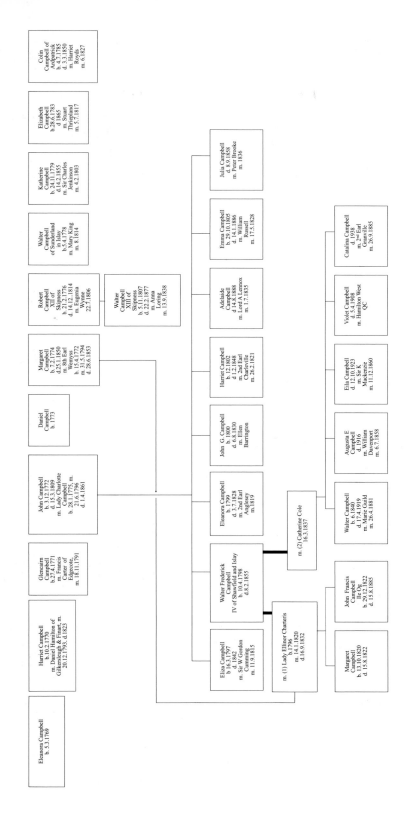

APPENDIX 1

Key Members of the Campbells of Skipness, Shawfield and Islay, 1600-1900

APPENDIX 2

Discovery of the Shawfield Manuscript

It is fortunate that there is in existence, a record of a number of Daniel's early trading activities. These are to be found in the Shawfield Manuscript,* a large archive containing many of Daniel's first business papers. It includes instructions to his captains, insurance of cargoes, bills, loans and letters from his agents in various parts of the world. The papers run from the earliest days of his trading life in 1691, until they come to an end in 1717. The greater part of the manuscript covers the late 1690s and the early years of the eighteenth century. It is a great pity that there are no documents from the second half of his life, since he was active through the 1720s and 1730s, although by that time he had made his fortune and may well have limited his principal activities to lending money, usually secured against land.

Daniel's great-great-grandson, John Francis Campbell, the famous Scottish folklorist, was most disappointed by the Shawfield Manuscript. It is perfectly true that the papers contain no mention of the Act of Union, the Darien Disaster,† the Equivalent or his parliamentary life, nor is there anything to indicate that he was a close friend of Robert Walpole. Such omissions are certainly frustrating, but the manuscript still provides us with a rich archive of material, with its detailed descriptions of maritime trade and its attendant difficulties. It is, perhaps, something of a ragbag of papers, but a fascinating social commentary on Scottish maritime life at the time.

The papers had evidently been long forgotten when, in January 1830, Lady Ellinor Campbell, John Francis' mother, opened a curious old strong box stored in a garret at Woodhall, the family seat in Lanarkshire. The box was found to contain a large number of papers; a note attached to one bundle tells that some letters had been removed and taken to 'Charles Sharpe'. I think that this man must have been a dealer in autograph letters who simply extracted those he thought the most significant and valuable. A note was made by John Francis Campbell 'a representative of Charles Sharpe has been written to and has promised to send anything which she may have'... but there is no family record of anything being returned.

The papers were then stored in the library at Woodhall. Following Lady Ellinor's death in 1832,‡ the family spent little time at Woodhall and someone, perhaps her widower, Walter, eventually took a part of the collection to Islay. There they were again forgotten for some years. Those left behind at Woodhall were sent to John Francis in London in 1847 following the sequestration of the estate.

In 1861 John Ramsay of Kildalton, who had bought part of the Islay estate following the family's bankruptcy in 1847, was 'warming' Islay House preparatory to the arrival of new tenants, when the chimney caught fire owing to a number of birds' nests inside it. Part of the house burned, but Ramsay managed to save some of the contents, including two sacks of papers that he sent to London, where they remained in John Francis' cellar for several years.

It was not until 1866 that he began the difficult job of sorting them. He enlisted the help of a man from the 'Stationery Office', presumably the HMSO, and noted that the work involved was equivalent to being secretary to a small Government department—'the pay is nothing and the results so far remarkably small'.§ John Ramsay is also thought to have stored papers connected with Islay in a warehouse in Edinburgh that apparently burned down too. In any event, although the manuscript may not give us much in the way of family history, it gives us a very good idea as to how Daniel made his fortune.

Somehow, the remains of the manuscript came into the possession of a Sir John Ramsden who lived in Gerrards Cross. Following his death, his library and papers were sent for sale by auction. The papers fetched £21,000 and were bought by the Mitchell Library in Glasgow.

---

* Shawfield Manuscript, Mitchell Library, Glasgow.

† It seems probably that letter 122 from St Eustatia refers to people from Caledonia as Darien was known.

‡ It appears that she suffered a mental illness.

§ Shawfield MS, handwritten summary of Daniel's voyages, Glasgow City Archives, ref. TD1022, R.F. Dell Papers. .

Summary of Trading Voyages
from the Shawfield Manuscript

The following two pages summarising Daniel's voyages (TD1022/8) were compiled by R.F. Dell while a member of the staff of Glasgow City Archives and Strathclyde Regional Archives. The manuscript reference is TD1619.

The facsimiles are reproduced with the kind permission of Glasgow City Archives and Special Collections.

Daniel Campbell, s. of laird of Skipness. m. Margaret Leckie, Glasgow, 1703.* 1/31.

Date	Entry	Ref
1692.	Two Brothers in America	
	Purchase of ship in Boston. Steven & Stanbury.	1/35, 1/31, 1/38, 1/37.
1693-4	Prosperous letter, purch. Boston. 1/41. 1/44, 1/45, 1/67, 1/64-5, 1/66.	
1692-3	Sales of (linen) cloth in Boston	1/32, 33.
1693	Thomas Irving to D. Campbell & John McGown, trade to Boston	1/70.
1693	Antelope, Boston, later Adventure of Glasgow: voyages.	1/49, 73.
1694	Owners of the Antelope. Caleb Hobart. Maryland to John Hill, London.	1/71, 1/69.
	John Borland & Co., Boston. Borland & Carter of Boston	1/72, 73.
1694	Adventure Glasgow voyages.	1/59, 60, 62.
1695	John Murhead's part. 1/80 1/63.	87, 146.
1695	Lily of London account at London: Letter re freighting. Pennsylvania	1/86, 91, 83, 84.
1696	Instructions for purchase of a ship in Boston. 1/101.	1/74, 75.
1696	Compensation for war losses	1/108, 109,
1697	Henry of Glasgow, trading to Bordeaux. 1/128. 1/126-7. 1/190 1/105.	1/113-118.
1696-7	Butter shipped to Amsterdam.	1/134
	Difficulty of wool sales in Hamburg.	1/125
1698	Calculations re cargo at St Kitts.	2/595
1697	Magdalene of Greenock - French wine	1/129.
1699	Calculations re cargo at St. Kitts.	1/122-123.
1699	Daniel buys Ard.'s ¼ share in Adventure	1/119.
"	Same	1/189.
1700	Tobacco imported in Elizabeth of Liverpool	1/173.
1697	Charter of Dispatch of London to Leeward Islands. etc.	1/147, 148. 181.
	Daniel & Archd. in partnership with Jas & Michael Coulterkreath.	
1697	John McMillen of Dunmore apprenticed to D.C. as merchant.	1/135.
1697	Wines in Port Glasgow	1/145.
1695-7	William & Thomas of London, John Smellie's a/c. James Montgomerie	1/132. 1/200
1699	Lyon linen cargo.	1/166.
1694	Elizabeth & Judith. Liverpool - Madeira.	1/168.
1700	Sugar shipped in Four Sisters, London. to Sam. Bali.	1/194. 195
c1700	Maria in wine trade. account.	1/212.
1701	Trade with Virginia.	1/214.
1700	News from Plymouth.	1/191.
1701	Sales of linen & herrings etc in West Indies	1/209.
1702	Alexander Campbell to N.Y.	1/239.
1702	Recovery of ship in Leewards.	1/235.
1702	Hopewell of Dublin, James Crosse, supercargo.	1/241
1701-2	Dove, fetch for Jamaica	1/240.
1703	James Waldinshaw & partners - sugar sold in Liverpool.	1/250
1703	Butter imports	1/267.
1703-5	Daniel Campbell H.M. Collector of Customs, Port Glasgow.	
1704	Lisbon imports in Sasauna	1/280.
1705-6	Neptune to Bordeaux.	2/355, 368, 357.
c1706	Voyage of Ester to Archangel	1/300
1707	Neptune, Clyde to Dublin & Proport. account	2/356, 358, 2/359, 362, 364, 2/360, 361, 363, 2/365, 373, 376, 370.
1707	Norwegian timber	2/381

* This date is wrong: Daniel married Margaret Leckie in 1695.

By now Daniel seems to be in partnership with Matthew Crawford.

Year	Description	Ref
1710	They take an apprentice in navigation.	2/469.
1707	Customs on brandy, Port Glasgow.	2/384.
		2/397.
1708	*Concord* of Glasgow to Livorno	
1708	*Susanna* of P.G. accounts. 2/412, 416. 396.	
	Bound Belfast to Barbadoes.	
1708	James Maxwell master of *London Galley* account. 2/406.	
1708-10	*London Galley* to Barbadoes. 2/422	2/398 399
	2/410. 2/446 451 455 462.	
1708	James Cougar's a/c of *London Galley* 2/414 2/403 103 2/408. 2/417	
1708	John Watt a/c of same. 2/421. 2/415. 2/411 2/413 2/409	
1709	Buying linen cloth from Matthew Atchison	2/418, 431.
	News from Virginia & Lisbon.	2/439. 440.
1710	*Expedition Galley* built in Boston for Matthew Crawford.	2/470.
1710	*Neptune* taken by the French 2/332, 345, 374.	2/466. 2/492
	Insurance from Virginia to Bristol. Henry Norris.	
1710	Cargo expenses.	2/475.
1710	Insurance from Baltic.	2/468.
	Ship built in Boston for Daniel Campbell. Robt to be master.	2/464, 467.
1710	Trading conditions in Madeira.	2/473.
1711	Employment of Matthew Campbell in Stockholm.	2/576.
	Union Galley & *American Merchant* for Virginia	2/501, 567.
	American Merchant tobacco to Bristol	2/511.
1711	Insurance of this ship. Henry Norris.	2/495, 496
	Vigilant's voyage	2/515, 566.
1711	Insurance on vessel plundered by French.	2/503.
	Expedition Galley, to Archangel.	2/516, 566, 683
1711	Insurance on this ship.	2/512, 513, 574
1711	*Union Galley* from Boston. Insurance	2/497, 504, 505 2/507, 508.
1712	Trade with Sweden.	2/509, 518
1712	*Vigilant's* cargo.	2/572, 573.
	Daniel in account with John Bowman	2/555.
1712	Sales of iron.	2/692.
	Iron from Sweden 2/498-9, 500, 490.	2/534, 565
1712	George & Elizabeth, William & many, iron from Stockholm.	2/579, 571, 570
	Campbell & Matthew Crawford	2/585-587.
1712	Iron from Stockholm, Russian Company	2/516, 517, 571
	Sea Flower with iron from Stockholm.	2/541, 569
1712	*Loyal Anne*, *William* + other ships. Iron imports.	2/574, 553
1712	Iron trade	2/584.
1711-13	Profit + expenses of Southern Sugar House.	2/564, 683.
1713	Thomas Hume to Daniel, from Livorno. re cargoes.	2/610.
1714	Herring trade Gothenburg.	2/679, 612.
	Interrogatories re cargoes.	2/688
1713	*St. George*, *Loyal Anne*. Iron from Stockholm.	2/581
1713	*Thorogood Sammes*, iron from Stockholm.	2/583.
1719	*Houston Galley* cork to Madeira + Antigua	2/582.
1724	Irish trade	2/354.
1727	*Neptune's* voyages.	2/375.

APPENDIX 4

Inventory of Goods found after the Shawfield Riots

This information has been taken from Transactions of the Glasgow Archaeological Society, No. XX1V) with the view that it is of considerable interest as a social document describing household possessions in a gentleman's house of that period.

The objects had been taken for safe keeping by various neighbours: Alexander Dunlop, Alexander Dicks, Duncan Campbell, In 'T' House, John Meek, Alexander Dunlop Wright. The six foolscap pages of the original document were all witnessed by Baillies Peter Murdoch and Robert Alexander; James Anderson and Mrs Margaret Somervell, Personal Maid to Lady Katherine Campbell, wife of Daniel.

One should also bear in mind that the Shawfield Mansion was just one of Daniel's houses.

Silver work in Mr Alexander Dunlop's:

Two large salvers made by James Luke
A small salver made by James Luke
Two large salvers having upon them a Cran for a Crest*
Two salvers marked K.D. with a 'Cornet' above†
Four silver candlesticks, one pair snuffers, and small dish
A Devideing spoon made by James Luke‡
Four Salts Squair, having upon them a Griffen with a Sun in its paw§
Two round salts having a Cran upon them
Two casters with the same Crest
The head of a Caster of the same Sheap
A silver Basson and a Silver Pot both for Shaveing
A large coffee pot of Silver
A Sockett for Candlestick of Silver
A black Sheggareen Case Containing Six knives, Six forks, six Spoons¶
A Case containing one Doz. Dicert knives, twelve spoons, one doz. Forks

Body linens and Cloaths

Nine musline Cravats, five Camlet Do., Nineteen Stocks for Cravats, four slips of night Caps, three sute of head Cloaths, two pair of Rufles of the Ladies, Eleven Holland Shirts of Shawfields, three shirts of the Ladys and a Camlet hand Cloath, five Holland aprons and one musline one of the Ladys, three pair of mens threed Stockins, nine Dozen and five of Dornick** and Damica [damask] Naprie, eight Damica and Dornick Table Cloaths, two pair of Course Linnen Sheets, a Cutt of Course Linnen Cloath, two Silk pettiecoats ane Linne Codd ware, two white Silk pockets and a Gold Stithest breast, two pair of Shoes one Laced and the other Silk, ane ell and ane half of rid flannan, three years old truepoint, Two froks of Mrs Kettie's††, two mens coats of flannan, four Spinnell of Bletcht [bleached] yearn, ane Spinell and ane half of Green yearn, ane old mourning Scarff and new white Duncaster Stockins.

---

  * Lady Katherine had previously been married to Sir William Denham of Westshiels, who's family crest was a crane holding a stone in its left foot.
  † Katherine Denham.
  ‡ ? for gravy.
  § Crest of the Campbells of Shawfield and Islay.
  ¶ Sheggareen was shark's skin, rare and fashionable.
 ** Linen cloth with raised figures originally manufactured at Tournay.
 †† Catherine—Daniel and Lady Katherine's daughter.

In Mr James Spreull's Cellar*

A blunderbuss for a Coach the but of the stock yrof broke of ... Seventy three Cleus of worsett yearn, two heir of little wheele worsett thread, two hire of Courss yearn for Secks, a stone box, All in a Hampeer Creele, a fine Tuilt Satine Baskett full of Little necessssaries for a new Born Child, nine yeards or a Cutt of bletcht harn, The Ladies Carrying Chair, two Holland [linen fabric] shirts of Shawfields, a cutt of fine Linnen measuring ten ells, a piece of a Shewed frok of Mrs Kettie's, a piece of Skypt Holland night Gown with two Small Table napkins, a black Cloath pettie Coat of the Ladies, a Scarlet flanan pettie Coat and pair of Silk Jumps of the Ladies, three remnants of new Stuff, a Dutch Toy box for a Child, two velvet masks, a piece of fine white Damica for a Gown to the Lady, a floured Silk night Gown with a Green silk Lyning opened out. Two gowns of black and white Tabbie† opened out, a remnant of a yellow silk Tushie‡ a Lutestring§ night Gown opened out, a remnant of Stript Lutestring, the old remnant of yello ditto, a remnant of rid stript Holland, some old vellom, a pieice of white Silk gimp for a pettie Coat, a piece of rid and white Cotton Tabie,two peices of old silk, ane old feather muff with its Case. Item, a map of Bills of fare, three pair of womens Silk Stockins, four pair of worsett¶ stockins with Silk Gushets [inserts], some Cheapens of Silk gowns, three pieces of old black silk, ane piece of new black silk, three pieces of real hair for a wig, A pair of new Sandie collourred men's stockins, a remnant of Mrs Kettie's silk Tabie gown with some Cheapins of Calligo** and Silk, Some cheapens of rid and white Silk and Scarlet, one piece of Green and one piece of yellow Silk, Eight pieces more of reall hair for a wig, Eleven yards of fine Holland, four yrds and ane half white Calligo, in one piece, three other Lesser pieces, and one apron of the same, a box of Gum flouers, ane Damica Table napkins, with Lady's Torn Scarff and several other Silk things, a Trunk covered with Shelf skin marked with nails D.C. a pair of patons of the Ladies. A New Sadle, two holsters and two holster Caps, mounted with Gold, with tea†† Curple‡‡ and stirrup irons belonging thereto, a Tuilt Shewed Silk Case of Mrs. Kettie's, a Demi Sadle, covered wt Rushie leather, wanting all furniture, a Livery Coat of one of yr Servants, a pair of course sheets, and a ham and box with white soap.

In Mrs Campbells (Shawfield's Tennent) her House

Ane Livery Coat and vest Coat, ane Coat and vest Coat, Lyned with ridd, three paird of Servant's sheets, marked K.C.., three Cutt of Course linen Cloaoth, one Dozen of Dornick Naprie, one Damica Table Cloth, nine ell§§ of yellow Sarge,¶¶ fifteen ell of white Sarge, twelve Spinell and eighteen hire of Linnen yearn, Seventeen hesps*** of woollen yearn nineteen black and white worsett Cleus [balls of wool], two pair of colloured Shoes, two pair of colloured slipers, two houps, a Large Trunk Covered with self Skin, a pair of Silk and worsett stockins of yr Ladies, a stript silk gown of one of the Young Ladies, a Sute of new Cloaths of Shawfields viz. Coat, vest and Bretches.

In Northbarr's Lodging†††

A Green Gown and pettie Coat, trimed with Silver, a white Sheued Sattin Gown and pettie Coat, a yellow Tabie Gown and pettie coat, a yellow Tabie Gown and pettie Coat, lined with white; a black and white Lutstring gown and pettie coat, a white Calligo gown and pettie coat, Sheued with a White Crimstone linning, a Bragaad gown and pettiecoat lined with Scarlet, a Yellow Damase Gown and pettiecoat, a Garden stuff-night gown with a red ground, a bblack and white Norwich Crape night Gown, a Rid and white stript Satin night gown, a yellow Silk Tuilted (Quilted) petticoat, white silk, Tuilted pettie coat, a black marlie silk gown, a Bragaad

---

*   Spreull was a near neighbour.
†   Waved or watered silk with darker streaks.
‡   A girdle or belt.
§   A shiny, silk type fabric.
¶   Closely twisted yarn.
** Calico, plain cotton cloth.
†† An iron T-shaped item which hung from a horse's collar for attachment to the shafts of a carriage.
‡‡ Crupper to hold saddle in place by a loop going under the horse's tail.
§§ In Scotland, an ell measured 37.2 inches.
¶¶ A durable twilled, worsted cloth.
*** Hanks of yarn, a fourth part of a spindle.
††† Northbarr was probably a member of the Alexander family (J. Dalrymple Duncan).

silk pettiecoat not made up, the Tollet of the Dressing Table, a Calligo night gown, a black a short apron, a silk Tollet with four traps, a pair of Stays covered with white Silver Tabbie, a black breast of Tabbie a pair of Green silk shoes, Coat and vest Coast of white Cloath of Mr. John Campbell's.*

In Alex Dicks

Eleven fine Damize Table napkins marked K.D. and five ditto marked K.C. being in all Sixteen, one fine Dutch Damaze Table Cloath, a parcel Christening Cloaths viz the Ladys Tuilt Gown, a Childs Gown Tuilted, Cradle Cloath and Courtains Tuilted, a Childs Dust gown or tollet Satin bordered with Gold Lace, a box Containing a pair Childs shoes and stockins, a Child estcoat, a Shoulder Sheet, a Sueel belt,† two Shirts, a tippet, a Christening bub, a cross cloath, a pair of Child hand ruffles, a pair of Child Glovoeos, a side of bacon, a cutt of new Dornick or dyper, a broad with some blew Galloon on it.

In the House of Duncan Campbell, merchant at the Crose:

A Cutt of Servants sheeting, a Large Dornick Table cloath, Sixteen Dornick Table napkins, one fine Dornick Table Napkin unmade, a Course Tooll, ane Codware, anepair of Course Sheets; a Holland Shirt of Shawfields, a floured muslin apron of the Ladies ... three Calligo nightgowns, one Stript Holland night gown of young Ladies, a blew or Lead colloured Chinno Camlet for lyning a pettie coat, ane old blackspotted hood, a yellow silk hood of a rockle ane half bible of the Ladies, ane roll, ane rid ribbon.

In the house of Mrs Janet and Elizabeth Leckie:

Seven Cutt of Dornick for Table Napkins, Two Damize Table Cloaths not made, three broken knives with large silver hefts, four Dornick New table Napkins not made, one Dozen fine Table napkins, Six dozen ane half of fine Dornick Table napkins, a blew silk nightgown of Shawfields, two Cutt of fine broad linen for sheets, a pair of Dutch Holland sheets, A pair of linnen sheets, a white tuilt Sheued pettiecoat of the Ladies, a black Cloath gown of the Ladiesa black scarf and two black hoods of the same, a pair of yellow silk shoes of the same with silver lace on yem, a silk plaid of Mrs. Janets, a Stript black and white Tabie gown of ye Ladies, one Dutch Holland codware, two Cambrik and one musline Cravats of Shawfields w one stock, ane Holland shirt of Mr. Johns,‡ four ruffled shirts of Mr. Walters,§ two ditto of Skipness',¶ a Gold Tabie linen for a Gown of ye ladies, three short shirts of ditto, some whereof laced, two muslin tollets, two Dornick Table napkins more, Eight ells and ane half yellow silk moyhair new.

In the House of Mr James Anderson:

Ane Empty trunk, My Ladies Dressing plate viz. a Comb Box, a Ewart, two powder boxes, Two patch boxes, Two Comb brushes, Two egg potts, Two Caddell Cups with Covers, two long Cups with Covers, two brushes for Cloaths, a pin Cushan, two Candlesticks, a pair Snuffers and Snuff dish, The under part of a Caster, two boxes for wash balls, ane marrow spoon, ane old Silver spoon, the head of a Dressing Glass, four piece as the frame of said Glass all of Silver, ane Silver hilted Sword wanting the heek, Three Dornick Table napkins, ane yellow Gauss handkerchief embroidered, three tuilted Caps of Mrs. Ketties, ane fine fan Ivory and Tortoishell Spakes, ane Cambrik stock of Mr. Johns, a bout a qr of a yd of white three Damiz part of two papers of pins, a silver string for a watch, part of a white necklace most part of the beeds being lost, a Cambrick musline apron of the Ladies, a Litle silver box with a cornelian on the top having in it six Small Diamonds not sett, two pair Gold buttons philigraph, a little Straw box wherein is a Corall necklace and a Cornelian Seal Sett in Silver two Bibles one in 4to and the other in 8to both London print, a Bragaad vestcoat of Shawfields bordered wt silver and Gold Coast vestcoat and breeches of Mr. Walters not finished the Coat wanting a sleve, a Large new Bridle, a pair of Shawfields slippers, one pair Drogett breeches ane pair old black Cloath breeches thirteen Spinell and ane half Small worsett yearn

---

* John Campbell was Daniel Campbell's eldest son by his first marriage; he became a commissioner for the Inland Revenue.
† Swaddling bands.
‡ Daniel's eldest son.
§ His youngest son.
¶ Daniel's nephew, Colin, of Skipness who had married Daniel's daughter, Anne.

Peter Murdoch
Robt Alexander
Margret Somervell
James Anderson

I Mrs Margaret Somervell attendant to the Honble my Lady Shawfield Do hereby Declare that I have received the Goods mentioned in this and the five preceeding pages AND Wee Peter Murdoch and Robt Alexander merchants late Baillies in Glasgow and James Anderson Junior Merchant yr Do hereby Certifie that the sds Goods particularly above and within mentioned were truly Inventared by her at our Sight and presence In Testaimony whereof those pretts Consisting of this and the five preceeding pages (are written with ane other double thereof Subscrived be them of this date be James Kelburn Servt to John M'Gilchrist writer in Glasgow) and Subt Att Glasgow the third day of August Jaiviic and twenty five years before these witnesses John Muirhead Servitor to the South Sugar house of Glasgow and the sd James Kelburn

Peter Murdoch˙
Robt Alexander
James Anderson
Margret Somervell
John Muirhead Wittness
James Kelburn witness

---

*   Peter Murdoch was subsequently Provost of Glasgow in 1730-1.

APPENDIX 5

The Life and Career of Colin Campbell of Ardpatrick (1787–1858)

The youngest son of Walter Campbell of Shawfield and Islay, Colin of Ardpatrick had an interesting naval career. He served at Trafalgar as master's mate[*] on the *Defiance*, before working his way up to the rank of post captain. His naval career might have been more glorious had it not been for the defeat and imprisonment of Napoleon, which in turn led to the drastic diminuition in the size of the Royal Navy.[†] He served at the reduction of Martinique and Guadaloupe and has left a memorable account of a voyage to Peking.[‡] He sailed in late 1815 in the East Indiaman, *General Hewett*, skippered by his brother Captain Walter Campbell (of Sunderland in Islay), on the voyage to the Court of the Qing Emperor. It was on this voyage that Lord Amherst created a serious diplomatic incident by refusing to 'kowtow' to the Emperor. The *General Hewett* had been chartered from the East India Company to carry an impressive but inappropriate number of presents for the Emperor and additional supplies for the Royal Navy ships[§] transporting the embassy. However, the Emperor chose to keep only two pictures of the King and Queen and a painting of Doncaster races! The abortive expedition totally failed in its objective, which had been to obtain the Emperor's permission to open a mission in Peking and to be allowed to trade throughout China without the difficulties and harrassment to which foreign merchants had hitherto been subjected. The Emperor declared that the Chinese had no use for any of the merchandise brought from foreign countries.

Colin's own journal of the voyage is an extremely interesting work full of description of the places they visited and especially of their treatment at the hands of the various Chinese mandarins. Thanks to Lord Amherst's refusal to 'kowtow' which led to his dismissal by the Emperor without an audience, he, together with his vast suite, was forced to return overland to Canton—a trip that took four months. During this period, the *General Hewett* (called 'the tribute ship' by the Chinese) was refused permission to go up river to Whampoa, the port for Canton, to take on her return cargo, which left Colin and Walter kicking their heels someway down the river at what was referred to as the Second Bar. They were refused permission to go ashore or to receive visitors. Fortunately, their supercargo was well known to Walter from prevous voyages, and, on his frequent visits to supply the *General Hewett* with food supplies, he managed to smuggle in letters which he had sewn into the sails of his little boat, thus escaping the searches he was subjected to by the manadarins in their guard ships.

Walter eventually escaped to Canton in one of the ship's boats under cover of darkness, a fact which upset the mandarins on board the Chinese guard ships but which ultimately proved to be a bargaining tool for the English! The *Hewett* was kept captive from mid-September until she finally sailed for England at the beginning of January shortly after Lord Amherst reached Canton. Her route home included a stop at Java and then at St Helena where the Campbell brothers managed to catch a glimpse of her most famous prisoner, the deposed emperor Napoleon.

Colin died a rear admiral. His home, Ardpatrick, was finally sold in the 1920s by Colin's grandson Henry Hervey Campbell, another admiral, a very close personal friend of King George V and at one time, sailing master of the royal racing yacht *Britannia*. The sale of Ardpatrick severed the last family connection with Argyllshire.

---

[*] Aka midshipman.

[†] The letter he wrote home to his father, Walter Campbell, describing the action, has been published. The original is in the National Maritime Museum.

[‡] The log he kept of the journey is in the National Maritime Museum.

[§] HMS *Alceste* and HMS *Lyra*.

Bibliography

Principal MS Sources (series in parentheses)

Carmichael and Elliot processes, National Archives of Scotland (CS)
Clerk of Penicuik (GD18)
Coutts and Co. Archives
Archives of Drummonds Bank
Forfeited Estates Series E727, 728
Hamilton and Brandon papers, National Archives of Scotland (GD 406)
Houghton MS, Cambridge 'John Campbell to Robert Walpole, 29 June 1725
Kildalton Charter Chest papers, roll 918681, Glasgow City Archives (RH4)
Leven and Melville, National Archives of Scotland (GD26)
MP bundles, National Archives of Scotland (RH15)
Montrose Muniments, National Archives of Scotland (GD 220)
Mar & Kellie papers (GD124)
Shawfield papers, Mitchell Library, Glasgow
The Royal Bank of Scotland Archives (EQ)

Primary and Reference Sources and Local Archives

Airdrie Archives
Argyll & Bute Archives
Borough Records of Edinburgh, 1701-18
Calendar of Treasury Papers, 1708-14, vol. cvi, cvii; 1720-26; ccxxxiv, 1722
Cruickshanks, Handley and Hayton (ed.), *The House of Commons, 1690-1715*, CUP, 2002
Culloden Papers, British Library
Dictionary of National Biography
House of Commons Journal, 1725
Jerviswood 'Bannantyne Club, vol. I, pp. 4147-423, Edinburgh 1843, National Library of Scotland
Members of Parliament, Scotland 1359-1882, London 1882
Miscellany of the Abbotswood Club, vol. 1
National Archives Treasury Series
National Archives Colonial Series
North Lanarkshire Council, Museums & Heritage Section
RCAHMS, Argyll Inventory, extracts from vols 1, 2, 7, published 1997
Records of the Burgh of Glasgow, vol. iv, 1691-1717
Scottish Records Society, vols lvi, lx, vii, xxxv
State Papers Domestic, Geo. 1, The National Archives
Stockholm City Archives
Swedish National Archives
Young, M.D. (ed.), *The Parliaments of Scotland: Burgh and Shire Commissioners*, vol. I, Scottish Academic Press, 1992

Secondary Sources

Boyer, A., *Political State of Great Britain*, vol vii, April 1715

Brown, P. Hume, *The Union of 1707*, Glasgow, 1907

Brown, P. Hume, *The History of Scotland*, vol iii, Cambridge University Press, 1909

Campbell of Airds, Alastair, *History of Clan Campbell*, vol. iii, Edinburgh University Press, 2004

Campbell, Lord Archibald, *Records of Argyll*, William Blackwood, Edinburgh, 1885

Campbell, Colen, *Vitruvius Britannicus*, vol. ii, 1715

Cowan, E.J., 'Montrose and Argyll, 'The Scottish Nation, BBC 1972' ed. G. Menzie

Coxe, W. (ed.), *Memoirs of Sir Robert Walpole*, 1700-30 (vol. ii), republished by Kessinger, 2006

Cregreen, E., *The Changing Role of the House of Argyll in the Scottish Highlands*, Edinburgh, 1970

Cruft, Kittie, 'The Enigma of Woodhall House' in *Design and Practice in British Architecture*, vol. 27, 1984

Daiches, David, *Scotland and Union*, John Murray, 1977

Defoe, Daniel, *Tour through Great Britain in 1705*, 1706

Devine, T.M., *The Scottish Nation*, Penguin, 1999

Devine, T.M. and Jackson, Gordon, *History of Glasgow*, vol. I, Manchester, 1995

Fergusson, James, *Argyll in the '45*, London, 1951

Fremantle, Anne (ed.), *Journals of Elisabeth Wynne*, Oxford University Press, 1940

Glasgow Herald, 'New Light on old Glasgow', 1, 2 and 3 June 1959

Glimpses of old Glasgow, John Menzies, 1893

Graham, Angus, *Skipness, Memories of a Highland Estate*, Edinburgh, 1993

Graham, Eric, *A Maritime History of Scotland 1650-1700*, Tuckwell, 2002

Healey, Edna, *Coutts and Co., Portrait of a Private Bank, 1692-1992*, Hodder, 1992

Jupp, Clifford, *The History of Islay*, Museum of Islay Life, 2004

Kent, H.S.K., *War and Trade in Northern Seas*, Cambridge, 1973

Lamont, W., *Early History of Islay*, Glasgow, 1966

Lenman, B., *The Jacobite Risings in Britain, 1689-1745*, Scottish Cultural Press, 1995

Macarthur , W.F., *History of Port Glasgow*, Glasgow, 1932

McGeachy, Robert, *Argyll 1730-1850*, John Donald, 2005

Macgregor, *A History of Glasgow*, Glasgow, 1881

MacIntyre, D., *The Privateers*, London, 1975

Menary, G., *Life and letters of Duncan Forces of Culloden*, London, 1936

Miller, H.B. and A.H. (ed.), *The History of Cumbernauld and Kilsyth*, 1715, 1745, 1980

Mitchison, R., *The Government and the Highlands, 1707-1745*, Edinburgh, 1970

Mitchison, R. (ed.), *Why Scottish History Matters*, Saltire Society, 1997

Montagu, Lady Mary Wortley, *Letters*, London, 1906

Munro, N., *History of The Royal Bank of Scotland, 1727-1927*, Edinburgh, 1928

Murray, D., *The York Building Company*, Edinburgh, 1973

Nash, R., *Scottish Economic Review*, series ii, xxxvi, 1982

Nash, R., *Economic History Review*, series ii, xxxvi, 1982

Plumb, J., *Sir Robert Walpole*, London, 1960

Prebble, John, *The Darien Disaster, the Scottish Dream of Empire*, Edinburgh, 1968

Price, J.M., 'The Rise of Glasgow in the Chesapeake Tobacco Trade, 1707-1775', *William and Mary Quarterly*, series iii, vol. 11, 1954

Rae, T. (ed.), *The Union of 1707*, Blackie, 1974

Ramsay, F. (ed.), *The Day Book of Daniel Campbell of Shawfield, 1767*, Aberdeen University Press, 1991

Russell, Constance, *Three Generations of Fascinating Women*, Longmans Green, London, 1903

Saville, R., *The Bank of Scotland, 1695-1995*, Edinburgh, 1996

Shaw, John Stuart, *The Political History of 18th century Scotland*, Macmillan, 1999

Sinclair, Sir John (ed.), *Statistical Account of Scotland*, Edinburgh, 1794

Smith, G.G., *The Book of Islay*, Edinburgh, 1794

Smith, Gavin D., *The Scottish Smuggler*, Birlinn, 2003

Smout, T., 'The Glasgow Merchant Community', *Scottish Historical Review*, vol. 6, 1968

Smout, T., *Scottish Trade on the Eve of Union*, Edinburgh, 1963

Stevenson, T., *Argyle Papers*, privately published

Storrie, Margaret, *Islay, Biography of an Island*, OA Press, 1981

Sunter, Ronald, *Patronage and Politics in Scotland, 1707-1832*, Edinburgh, 1986

Szechi, Daniel (ed.), *George Lockart of Carnwath*, Tuckwell Press, 2002

Tayler, H., 'John Duke of Argyll', *Scottish Historical Review*, vol. xxvi

Taylor, G. Stirling, *Robert Walpole*, Jonathan Cape, 1931

Terry, C.S., *Jacobites and the Union*, Cambridge, 1922

Todd, G. Eyre, *History of Glasgow'*, vol. 3, Glasgow, 1934

Whately, Christopher, *The Scots and the Union*, Edinburgh University Press, 2006

Wodrow, Robert, *Analecta*, 1728

Index

Act of Security, 32
Act of Settlement, 32
Adolphus Frederick, King of Sweden, 64
Agen, 15
Aird, John, 43, 60
Aiton, William 59
Alien Act (1705), 32
Alison, Mrs Peggy, 26
Andersons, writers to the *Signet* in
   Edinburgh, 81, 82
Andrew & Jonathan Belcher, shipbuilders,
   Boston, 14
Anne, Queen (1702–1714), 32, 33
Anstruther, Sir Alexander of Newark, 40
Archangel, 15
Ardentinnie, 17
Argyll *see* Campbell
Armour, John, 73
Ashton, John of Goteborg, 63
Atholl, Marquis of, 1, 5, 33
Attenbury Plot (1722), 79

Baillie of Jerviswood, George, 34
Bank of Scotland, 25, 48, 50, 61
Beaujolais, Louis Charles d'Orleans, Comte
   de, 93, 94
Bedoire, Frans, 63
Bedoire, Jean, 63
Bedoire, Magdalena, wife of Robert
   Campbell of Stockholm, 63
Bellamont, Earl of, 22, 23
Blackwood, John, 45
Bonnie Prince Charlie (Prince Charles
   Edward), 62, 77, 78, 86, 87
Bordeaux, 15
Borland, Rev. Francis, 21
Bothwell Church, 88
Bowman, Provost, 43, 44
Bowmore, Islay, 84, 90, 91, 92, 93
Broderick, Thomas, 66
Buchan, David Earl of, 54
Bury, Rev. Edward John, 93
Bushell, Captain Francis, 69, 70, 74
Bute, Earl of, 14

Cahors, 15
Campbell, Agnes, 2nd wife Matthew of
   Orgaig, 14n
Campbell, Alexander of Cawdor (d. 1697),
   81
Campbell, Angus (1660-1731), Captain of
   Skipness, brother to Daniel, 2, 43
Campbell, Anne (daughter of Daniel),
   married her cousin, Colin of Skipnes, 42-4
Campbell, Archibald, 1st Duke of Argyll (d.
   1703), 35
Campbell, Archibald of Jura, 85
Campbell, Lord Archibald, 95
Campbell, Lady Charlotte, 46, 93
Campbell, Colen, architect, 57, 58, 60
Campbell, Colin (d. 1685), uncle to Daniel,
   1, 3, 4
Campbell, Colin (1690-1756), Captain
   of Skipness, nephew to Daniel, son of
   Angus, 87, 88, 110
Campbell, Colin (1711–1739), nephew to
   Daniel, son of brother John, 17
Campbell, Admiral Colin of Ardpatrick
   (1785–1850), great-grandson of Daniel,
   95, 115
Campbell, Colin of Blytheswood, 45, 49
Campbell, ('Great') Daniel of Shawfield &
   Islay (c.1670-1753), known as 'Donald' in
   his youth, 1, 2, 3
   Darien Scheme, 19, 21, 22, 24
   death, 88
   employment by Customs, 25-30, 65, 67
   friendship with Walpole, 41, 42, 45
   involvement in politics and the Union,
   31, 34, 35, 37-41, 43-6
   maritime trading, 5-17
   properties:
     Woodhall, 55-9, 67, 73;
     Shawfield, Rutherglen, 40, 55;
     Shawfield Mansion, Glasgow, 57, 59,
      60, 67, 70;
     Kilsyth, 60, 61, 62, 87, 91;
     Island of Islay, 58, 79, 81-6, 90
   Shawfield (Malt Tax) Riots, 66, 69, 70,
     72, 74-9

Campbell, Daniel the Younger of Shawfield and Islay, grandson of Great Daniel (c.1737-1777), 58, 83, 84, 87, 88, 89, 91
Campbell, Dugald of Kilberrie, 8, 15, 16, 29
Campbell of Glenure, 87
Campbell, Harriet Beaujolais (b. 1770), great-grandaughter of Great Daniel, 91, 93
Campbell, Sir Hugh of Cawdor (d. 1717), father of Alexander, 81, 85
Campbell, James, merchant of London, 23
Campbell, Sir James of Auchinleck, 62
Campbell, Jarrett and Dobson, Stockholm, 14
Campbell, Jean of Ballmeanach, mother of Daniel, 82
Campbell, John Francis of Islay, great-great-great-grandson of Daniel (1822-1885), 17, 98, 101
Campbell, John (1664-1739), brother of Daniel, 2, 7, 26, 46, 66, 73, 74
Campbell, John (1696-1746), son of Daniel, 40, 76, 83, 86, 87, 110
Campbell, John (d. 1773), grandson to Daniel, 46
Campbell, John of Kilberrie, aka 'of the Black River', Jamaica, 21
Campbell, John, banker (later Coutts and Co), 14, 50, 51, 52
Campbell, John of Cawdor (d. 1777), son of Alexander, 81, 82, 83
Campbell, John of Deptford, 23
Campbell, John of Mamore, Chamberlain to Duke of Argyll, 17, 29, 86
Campbell, John, 2nd Duke of Argyll, 25, 31, 35, 42, 51, 60, 71, 83
Campbell, Katherine (b. 1715), daughter of Daniel, 55
Campbell, Katherine (1779-1855), great-grandaughter of Daniel, 91
Campbell, Capt. Lachlan, 84
Campbell, Margaret (1774-1850), wife of Francis, 8th Earl of Wemyss, 91
Campbell, Marion of Kilberrie, 16
Campbell, Capt. Matthew of Orgaig (1672-1721), brother of Daniel 2, 9, 10, 13, 14, 25, 44, 46, 51
Campbell, Robert of Skipness (1776-1814), 88, 93, 94, 95
Campbell, Robert of Stockholm (1688-1761), half-brother of Daniel, 2, 14, 15, 63
Campbell, Robert, Dean of Guild, Glasgow, 57
Campbell, Col. Robert (b. c.1714), son of Robert of Stockholm), 63
Campbell, Walter (1640-1702), Captain of Skipness, father of Daniel, 1, 2, 4

Campbell, Walter (1698-1732), son of Daniel, 54
Campbell, Walter (1741-1815), grandson of Daniel, 91, 92, 93
Campbell, Walter Frederick (1798-1855), of Shawfield and Islay, great-great-grandson of Daniel, 96, 97, 98, 100
Campbell, Walter (b. 1778), of Sunderland in Islay, great-grandson of Daniel, 92
Campbell, Walter of Skipness, son of Robert of Skipness, 95
Campbell, William, 46
Carmichael, Lord, 24
Cedecreutz, Comtesse Maria, daughter of Robert of Stockholm, 63, 64
Chapin, Ebeneezer, 9
Charles II, 19, 32
Charles Edward, Prince (Bonnie Prince Charlie) 77, 78
Charteris, Lady Ellinor (1796-1832), wife of Walter Frederick, 96
Clerk, Sir John of of Penicuik, 66
Clochfin, 17
Cockburn, Adam, 35
Cockpit, Whitehall, 35, 36
Colzium House, Kilsyth, 62
Company trading to Africa and the Indies, 19, 22, 23
Corson, Alexander, 55
Coutts & Co., 50
Crauford, Laurence of Jordanhill, 55
Crawford, Matthew, 14, 50
Crosse, James, Supercargo 12
Cunningham, Lady Henrietta, 54

Dalrymple, Sir Hugh, 35
Darien, 17, 19, 20, 21, 23, 24, 33, 37, 48
Daschkow, Princess Ekaterina Roumanovia, 89
Defoe, Daniel, 33
Delahaye, Charles, 71
Deloraine, Lord, 75
Denholm (Denham), Sir William Bt, 54
Denholm, Lady Katherine, second wife of Daniel 54, 55, 62
Dixon, Sir Robert, 29, 30
Drummond, Andrew, 52
Drummond, George, 53, 76
Drummond, Robert, 21, 22
Drummond, Thomas, 21, 22, 23
Drummonds Bank, 50, 52
Dundas, Robert of Arniston, 35, 66, 72, 74
Duplin, Viscount, 35

Edmonstone, Sir Archibald, 91

Equivalent, The, 48, 49, 50, 51, 52, 53
Erskine, James of Grange, 76

Finlaggan, Islay, 80
Fletcher, Andrew of Saltoun, 34, 38
Florence, 15
Forbes, Duncan of Culloden, 66, 68, 70
Forfar, Earl of, 50

George I, Elector of Hanover, 32, 33
George II, 38
Glasgow, Earl of, 35, 42, 50
Glassford, John, 78
Glassford Street, 78
Glencairn, Earl of, 54
Glencoe, 31
Godfrey, Michael, 48
Gordon, Thomas of Earlston & Airds, m. Katherine daughter of Daniel, 55
Graham, Mungo of Gorthie, 44, 46, 54
Grant, Alexander of that Ilk, 49
Gray, Sir James, 37
Guinea, 12, 13, 16, 51

Hamilton, Duke of, 3, 23, 33, 34, 35, 38, 39
Hamilton, Dowager Duchess of, 21, 35, 40
Hamilton, Lord Basil, 24
Harley, Robert, 33
Hodges, James, 37
Holytoun, 57
Home, Earl of, 34
Howell, Capt. John, 11, 12, 22

Islay (Ilay), Earl of, 25, 51, 65, 70, 74
Islay House, 85, 91, 96
Islay, Island of, 47, 58, 79, 80

James II and VII, 1
Jarrett, John, 14
Johnston, Sir Patrick, 35
Jura, Island of, 80, 81, 82, 85, 92

Kerr, Eleanor (d. 1785), wife of Walter Campbell grandson of Daniel, 88, 91
Kerr, Captain John, 11
Kew Gardens, 59
Kilbrennan, 88, 95
Kildalton, Islay, 92
Kildarrow, Islay, 83, 84, 85
Kilsyth Estate, 61, 91
Kilsyth, the Viscount (Livingston), 61, 62
Kintyre, 2, 82

Landi, Ottavio, 15
Leckie, Elizabeth, wife of John Campbell

brother of Daniel, 46
Leckie, John, father-in-law to Daniel, 10, 26, 46
Leckie, Margaret, 1st wife of Daniel, 10, 54
Leckie, Michael, brother of Margaret, 54
Leckie, William, 54
Leghorn (Livorno), 16
Livingston see Kilsyth
Lochindaal, Islay, 84
Lockhart, George of Carnwarth, 34, 38, 66, 69, 77, 79
Lot River, 15
Loudon, Earl of, 35
Louisa Ulrika, Queen of Sweden, 64
Luke, Robert, jeweller, 73

McDowall, Col. William, 77, 78
Maclean, Archibald, 28
Madeira, 15
Malt Tax riots see Shawfield Riots
Mann, Robert, 40, 41
Mar, the Earl of, 33, 38
Melville, Lord, 7
Middleton, George, 50, 52
Miller, Provost of Glasgow, 69, 70
Mitchell, James, Dean of Guild, 70
Montague, Charles, 48
Montgomerie, Francis, 35
Montgomerie, Hugh, 35, 50
Montgomerie, John, 40
Montrose, James Duke of, 3, 33, 34, 39, 42, 46
Morrison, Charles, 99, 100
Morrison, James, 100
Morrison, William, 35
Morthland, Professor Charles, 54
Morton, Earl of, 35
Murray, Richard, 29

Nanfan, John, 22, 23
Navigation Acts, 7
New York, 21, 22
Nicholson, Gov. of Maryland, 8
Nisbet, Mary, 2nd wife of Walter Campbell grandson of Daniel, 91
Noble, Robert, 29
Norris, Henry, 14, 16
Northesk, Earl of, 50
Nottingham, Earl of, 7

Ogilvie, Sir Alexander of Forglen, 35
Orkney, Earl of, 23

Panama, 12, 19
Paterson, William, 19, 21, 48

Penicuick, Capt. Robert, 21
Playfair, William, 96
Port Askaig, Islay, 80
Port Charlotte, Islay, 96
Port Ellen, Islay, 96
Port Leven, 11
Port Po (Italy), 15
Port Wemyss, Islay, 96

Queensberry, The Duke of, 10, 33, 37

Ramsay, John, 97, 100
Ricart, Sir Paul, 20
Robison, James, Supercargo, 9, 10
Rodgers, Robert, 30, 39, 42
Ronald, James, 28
Rooke, Commander George, 7
Rosebery, Earl of, 35
Ross, Lord, 35
Roxburghe, Duke of, 34, 74
Royal Bank of Scotland, The, 49, 53
Royal Hospital, Chelsea, 41, 42

St Eustatia (The Golden Rock), 11
St Kitts (St Christopher), 11, 15
St Malo, 11
Scott, Sir Walter, 36
Seafield, Earl of, 13, 35
Seton, Sir William, 17, 35
Shawfield, Rutherglen, 39, 40, 47, 55, 91
Shawfield Mansion, Trongate, Glasgow, 57,
    59, 60, 66, 75
Shawfield Riots, 67-79
Ships:
    Adventure, 10, 11, 12, 22, 23
    Aime Mary, 14
    Caledonia, 12, 21, 22
    Concorde, 16
    Dumbarton Castle, 13, 14
    Eagle Galley, 27
    Endeavour, 21, 22
    Expedition Galley, 14
    Happy Entrance of Dublin, 14
    Hopewell, 12
    Houston Galley, 16
    James, 10, 11
    Jannet, 9
    Lillie, 11
    Mayflower, 27
    Neptune, 15, 27
    Pelican, 7
    Prosperous, 9, 10

    Royal Mary, 14
    Royal William, 14
    St Andrew, 7, 21
    St Peter and St Paul, 14
    Unicorn, 21, 23
Skipness Castle, Kintyre, 1, 2, 43, 87, 93, 94
Smith, James, architect, 59
Smith, Thomas, 29, 42
Smollett, Sir James of Bonhill, 35
Somervell, Mrs, 108
Sophia, Electress of Hanover, 32
South Sea Bubble, 52, 63
Spooner, Abraham, 14
Stair, Earl of, 71
Stark, James, 61
Steuart, Robert of Tillicoulty, 35
Stewart, Allen Breac, 87
Stewart, Daniel, 35
Stewart, James of Glenure, 87
Stirling, James, 43
Storey, Rowland, 9
Sugar houses, 12, 13, 51
Sunderland in Islay, 92
Sutherland, Earl of, 35

Townshend, Lord, 43, 67, 71, 72
Turnbull, William, 73
Tweeddale, Marquis of, 20, 34

Wade, General, 67, 73, 80
Wafer, Lionel, 20, 21
Walker, William, 13
Walkinshaw, Clementina, 78
Walkinshaw, John, 78
Walkinshaw, Katherine, 62
Walpole, Sir Robert, 2, 38, 40, 41, 45, 53,
    56, 60, 66, 71, 73, 74, 79
Wemyss, Francis 8th Earl of, 35, 91
Wessel, Peter, 22
Whitehaven, Port of, 7
Whitelaw, Alexander, 101
William III, 20, 24, 31, 32
Wisheart, William, 45
Wodrow, Rev. Robert, 45, 66, 71, 76
Woodhall House, Lanark, 4, 47, 55, 56, 67,
    76, 89, 100
Wortley Montague, Lady Mary, 41
Wynne, Eugenia, married Robert Campbell
    of Skipness, 93, 94

York Building Company, 60, 61